NORWEGIAN
VOCABULARY

FOR ENGLISH SPEAKERS

ENGLISH-
NORWEGIAN

The most useful words
To expand your lexicon and sharpen
your language skills

3000 words

Norwegian vocabulary for English speakers - 3000 words
By Andrey Taranov

T&P Books vocabularies are intended for helping you learn, memorize and review foreign words. The dictionary is divided into themes, covering all major spheres of everyday activities, business, science, culture, etc.

The process of learning words using T&P Books' theme-based dictionaries gives you the following advantages:

- Correctly grouped source information predetermines success at subsequent stages of word memorization
- Availability of words derived from the same root allowing memorization of word units (rather than separate words)
- Small units of words facilitate the process of establishing associative links needed for consolidation of vocabulary
- Level of language knowledge can be estimated by the number of learned words

T&P Books Publishing
www.tpbooks.com

ISBN: 978-1-78492-014-2

This book is also available in E-book formats.
Please visit www.tpbooks.com or the major online bookstores.

NORWEGIAN VOCABULARY
for English speakers

T&P Books vocabularies are intended to help you learn, memorize, and review foreign words. The vocabulary contains over 3000 commonly used words arranged thematically.

* Vocabulary contains the most commonly used words
* Recommended as an addition to any language course
* Meets the needs of beginners and advanced learners of foreign languages
* Convenient for daily use, revision sessions, and self-testing activities
* Allows you to assess your vocabulary

Special features of the vocabulary

* Words are organized according to their meaning, not alphabetically
* Words are presented in three columns to facilitate the reviewing and self-testing processes
* Words in groups are divided into small blocks to facilitate the learning process
* The vocabulary offers a convenient and simple transcription of each foreign word

The vocabulary has 101 topics including:

Basic Concepts, Numbers, Colors, Months, Seasons, Units of Measurement, Clothing & Accessories, Food & Nutrition, Restaurant, Family Members, Relatives, Character, Feelings, Emotions, Diseases, City, Town, Sightseeing, Shopping, Money, House, Home, Office, Working in the Office, Import & Export, Marketing, Job Search, Sports, Education, Computer, Internet, Tools, Nature, Countries, Nationalities and more …

T&P BOOKS' THEME-BASED DICTIONARIES

The Correct System for Memorizing Foreign Words

Acquiring vocabulary is one of the most important elements of learning a foreign language, because words allow us to express our thoughts, ask questions, and provide answers. An inadequate vocabulary can impede communication with a foreigner and make it difficult to understand a book or movie well.

The pace of activity in all spheres of modern life, including the learning of modern languages, has increased. Today, we need to memorize large amounts of information (grammar rules, foreign words, etc.) within a short period. However, this does not need to be difficult. All you need to do is to choose the right training materials, learn a few special techniques, and develop your individual training system.

Having a system is critical to the process of language learning. Many people fail to succeed in this regard; they cannot master a foreign language because they fail to follow a system comprised of selecting materials, organizing lessons, arranging new words to be learned, and so on. The lack of a system causes confusion and eventually, lowers self-confidence.

T&P Books' theme-based dictionaries can be included in the list of elements needed for creating an effective system for learning foreign words. These dictionaries were specially developed for learning purposes and are meant to help students effectively memorize words and expand their vocabulary.

Generally speaking, the process of learning words consists of three main elements:

- Reception (creation or acquisition) of a training material, such as a word list
- Work aimed at memorizing new words
- Work aimed at reviewing the learned words, such as self-testing

All three elements are equally important since they determine the quality of work and the final result. All three processes require certain skills and a well-thought-out approach.

New words are often encountered quite randomly when learning a foreign language and it may be difficult to include them all in a unified list. As a result, these words remain written on scraps of paper, in book margins, textbooks, and so on. In order to systematize such words, we have to create and continually update a "book of new words." A paper notebook, a netbook, or a tablet PC can be used for these purposes.

This "book of new words" will be your personal, unique list of words. However, it will only contain the words that you came across during the learning process. For example, you might have written down the words "Sunday," "Tuesday," and "Friday." However, there are additional words for days of the week, for example, "Saturday," that are missing, and your list of words would be incomplete. Using a theme dictionary, in addition to the "book of new words," is a reasonable solution to this problem.

The theme-based dictionary may serve as the basis for expanding your vocabulary.

It will be your big "book of new words" containing the most frequently used words of a foreign language already included. There are quite a few theme-based dictionaries available, and you should ensure that you make the right choice in order to get the maximum benefit from your purchase.

Therefore, we suggest using theme-based dictionaries from T&P Books Publishing as an aid to learning foreign words. Our books are specially developed for effective use in the sphere of vocabulary systematization, expansion and review.

Theme-based dictionaries are not a magical solution to learning new words. However, they can serve as your main database to aid foreign-language acquisition. Apart from theme dictionaries, you can have copybooks for writing down new words, flash cards, glossaries for various texts, as well as other resources; however, a good theme dictionary will always remain your primary collection of words.

T&P Books' theme-based dictionaries are specialty books that contain the most frequently used words in a language.

The main characteristic of such dictionaries is the division of words into themes. For example, the *City* theme contains the words "street," "crossroads," "square," "fountain," and so on. The *Talking* theme might contain words like "to talk," "to ask," "question," and "answer".

All the words in a theme are divided into smaller units, each comprising 3–5 words. Such an arrangement improves the perception of words and makes the learning process less tiresome. Each unit contains a selection of words with similar meanings or identical roots. This allows you to learn words in small groups and establish other associative links that have a positive effect on memorization.

The words on each page are placed in three columns: a word in your native language, its translation, and its transcription. Such positioning allows for the use of techniques for effective memorization. After closing the translation column, you can flip through and review foreign words, and vice versa. "This is an easy and convenient method of review – one that we recommend you do often."

Our theme-based dictionaries contain transcriptions for all the foreign words. Unfortunately, none of the existing transcriptions are able to convey the exact nuances of foreign pronunciation. That is why we recommend using the transcriptions only as a supplementary learning aid. Correct pronunciation can only be acquired with the help of sound. Therefore our collection includes audio theme-based dictionaries.

The process of learning words using T&P Books' theme-based dictionaries gives you the following advantages:

• You have correctly grouped source information, which predetermines your success at subsequent stages of word memorization

• Availability of words derived from the same root (lazy, lazily, lazybones), allowing you to memorize word units instead of separate words

• Small units of words facilitate the process of establishing associative links needed for consolidation of vocabulary

• You can estimate the number of learned words and hence your level of language knowledge

• The dictionary allows for the creation of an effective and high-quality revision process

• You can revise certain themes several times, modifying the revision methods and techniques

• Audio versions of the dictionaries help you to work out the pronunciation of words and develop your skills of auditory word perception

The T&P Books' theme-based dictionaries are offered in several variants differing in the number of words: 1.500, 3.000, 5.000, 7.000, and 9.000 words. There are also dictionaries containing 15,000 words for some language combinations. Your choice of dictionary will depend on your knowledge level and goals.

We sincerely believe that our dictionaries will become your trusty assistant in learning foreign languages and will allow you to easily acquire the necessary vocabulary.

TABLE OF CONTENTS

PERSONAL INFORMATION. FAMILY 70

HUMAN BODY. MEDICINE 73

APARTMENT 80

THE EARTH. WEATHER 85

PRONUNCIATION GUIDE

Letter	Norwegian example	T&P phonetic alphabet	English example
Aa	plass	[a], [ɑː]	bath, to pass
Bb	bøtte, albue	[b]	baby, book
Cc [1]	centimeter	[s]	city, boss
Cc [2]	Canada	[k]	clock, kiss
Dd	radius	[d]	day, doctor
Ee	rett	[eː]	longer than in bell
Ee [3]	begå	[ɛ]	man, bad
Ff	fattig	[f]	face, food
Gg [4]	golf	[g]	game, gold
Gg [5]	gyllen	[j]	yes, New York
Gg [6]	regnbue	[ŋ]	English, ring
Hh	hektar	[h]	humor
Ii	kilometer	[ɪ], [i]	tin, see
Kk	konge	[k]	clock, kiss
Kk [7]	kirke	[h]	humor
Jj	fjerde	[j]	yes, New York
kj	bikkje	[h]	humor
Ll	halvår	[l]	lace, people
Mm	middag	[m]	magic, milk
Nn	november	[n]	name, normal
ng	id_langt	[ŋ]	English, ring
Oo [8]	honning	[ɔ]	bottle, doctor
Oo [9]	fot, krone	[u]	book
Pp	plomme	[p]	pencil, private
Qq	sequoia	[k]	clock, kiss
Rr	sverge	[r]	rice, radio
Ss	appelsin	[s]	city, boss
sk [10]	skikk, skyte	[ʃ]	machine, shark
Tt	stør, torsk	[t]	tourist, trip
Uu	brudd	[y]	fuel, tuna
Vv	kraftverk	[v]	very, river
Ww	webside	[v]	very, river
Xx	mexicaner	[ks]	box, taxi
Yy	nytte	[ɪ], [i]	tin, see
Zz [11]	New Zealand	[s]	star, cats
Ææ	vær, stær	[æ]	chess, man

Letter	Norwegian example	T&P phonetic alphabet	English example
Øø	ørn, gjø	[ø]	eternal, church
Åå	gås, værhår	[oː]	fall, bomb

Comments

[1] before e, i
[2] elsewhere
[3] unstressed
[4] before a, o, u, å
[5] before i and y
[6] in combination gn
[7] before i and y
[8] before two consonants
[9] before one consonant
[10] before i and y
[11] in loanwords only

ABBREVIATIONS
used in the vocabulary

English abbreviations

ab.	-	about
adj	-	adjective
adv	-	adverb
anim.	-	animate
as adj	-	attributive noun used as adjective
e.g.	-	for example
etc.	-	et cetera
fam.	-	familiar
fem.	-	feminine
form.	-	formal
inanim.	-	inanimate
masc.	-	masculine
math	-	mathematics
mil.	-	military
n	-	noun
pl	-	plural
pron.	-	pronoun
sb	-	somebody
sing.	-	singular
sth	-	something
v aux	-	auxiliary verb
vi	-	intransitive verb
vi, vt	-	intransitive, transitive verb
vt	-	transitive verb

Norwegian abbreviations

f	-	feminine noun
f pl	-	feminine plural
m	-	masculine noun
m pl	-	masculine plural
m/f	-	masculine, neuter
m/f pl	-	masculine/feminine plural
m/f/n	-	masculine/feminine/neuter

m/n	-	masculine, feminine
n	-	neuter
n pl	-	neuter plural
pl	-	plural

BASIC CONCEPTS

1. Pronouns

I, me	jeg	['jæj]
you	du	[dʉ]
he	han	['hɑn]
she	hun	['hʉn]
it	det, den	['de], ['den]
we	vi	['vi]
you (to a group)	dere	['derə]
they	de	['de]

2. Greetings. Salutations

Hello! (fam.)	Hei!	['hæj]
Hello! (form.)	Hallo! God dag!	[hɑ'lʉ], [gʉ 'dɑ]
Good morning!	God morn!	[gʉ 'mɔːɳ]
Good afternoon!	God dag!	[gʉ'dɑ]
Good evening!	God kveld!	[gʉ 'kvɛl]
to say hello	å hilse	[ɔ 'hilsə]
Hi! (hello)	Hei!	['hæj]
greeting (n)	hilsen (m)	['hilsən]
to greet (vt)	å hilse	[ɔ 'hilsə]
How are you? (form.)	Hvordan står det til?	['vʉːdɑn stoːr de til]
How are you? (fam.)	Hvordan går det?	['vʉːdɑn gor de]
What's new?	Hva nytt?	[va 'nʏt]
Goodbye! (form.)	Ha det bra!	[hɑ de 'brɑ]
Bye! (fam.)	Ha det!	[hɑ 'de]
See you soon!	Vi ses!	[vi sɛs]
Farewell!	Farvel!	[far'vɛl]
to say goodbye	å si farvel	[ɔ 'si far'vɛl]
So long!	Ha det!	[hɑ 'de]
Thank you!	Takk!	['tɑk]
Thank you very much!	Tusen takk!	['tʉsən tɑk]
You're welcome	Bare hyggelig	['bɑrə 'hʏgeli]
Don't mention it!	Ikke noe å takke for!	['ikə 'nʉe ɔ 'takə fɔr]
It was nothing	Ingen årsak!	['iŋən 'oːʂak]
Excuse me! (fam.)	Unnskyld, ...	['ʉnˌʂyl ...]

| Excuse me! (form.) | Unnskyld meg, ... | ['ʉnˌsyl me ...] |
| to excuse (forgive) | å unnskylde | [ɔ 'ʉnˌsylə] |

to apologize (vi)	å unnskylde seg	[ɔ 'ʉnˌsylə sæj]
My apologies	Jeg ber om unnskyldning	[jæj ber ɔm 'ʉnˌsyldniŋ]
I'm sorry!	Unnskyld!	['ʉnˌsyl]
to forgive (vt)	å tilgi	[ɔ 'tilˌji]
It's okay! (that's all right)	Ikke noe problem	['ikə 'nʉe prʊ'blem]
please (adv)	vær så snill	['vær sɔ 'snil]

Don't forget!	Ikke glem!	['ikə 'glem]
Certainly!	Selvfølgelig!	[sɛl'følgəli]
Of course not!	Selvfølgelig ikke!	[sɛl'følgəli 'ikə]
Okay! (I agree)	OK! Enig!	[ɔ'kɛj], ['ɛni]
That's enough!	Det er nok!	[de ær 'nɔk]

3. Questions

Who?	Hvem?	['vɛm]
What?	Hva?	['va]
Where? (at, in)	Hvor?	['vʊr]
Where (to)?	Hvorhen?	['vʊrhen]
From where?	Hvorfra?	['vʊrfra]
When?	Når?	[nɔr]
Why? (What for?)	Hvorfor?	['vʊrfʊr]
Why? (~ are you crying?)	Hvorfor?	['vʊrfʊr]

What for?	Hvorfor?	['vʊrfʊr]
How? (in what way)	Hvordan?	['vʊːdɑn]
What? (What kind of ...?)	Hvilken?	['vilkən]
Which?	Hvilken?	['vilkən]

To whom?	Til hvem?	[til 'vɛm]
About whom?	Om hvem?	[ɔm 'vɛm]
About what?	Om hva?	[ɔm 'va]
With whom?	Med hvem?	[me 'vɛm]

How many?	Hvor mange?	[vʊr 'mɑŋə]
How much?	Hvor mye?	[vʊr 'mye]
Whose?	Hvis?	['vis]

4. Prepositions

with (accompanied by)	med	[me]
without	uten	['ʉtən]
to (indicating direction)	til	['til]
about (talking ~ ...)	om	['ɔm]

before (in time)	før	['før]
in front of ...	foran, framfor	['fɔran], ['framfɔr]
under (beneath, below)	under	['ʉnər]
above (over)	over	['ɔvər]
on (atop)	på	['pɔ]
from (off, out of)	fra	['fra]
of (made from)	av	[aː]
in (e.g., ~ ten minutes)	om	['ɔm]
over (across the top of)	over	['ɔvər]

5. Function words. Adverbs. Part 1

Where? (at, in)	Hvor?	['vʊr]
here (adv)	her	['hɛr]
there (adv)	der	['dɛr]
somewhere (to be)	et sted	[et 'sted]
nowhere (not anywhere)	ingensteds	['iŋən,stɛts]
by (near, beside)	ved	['ve]
by the window	ved vinduet	[ve 'vindʉə]
Where (to)?	Hvorhen?	['vʊrhen]
here (e.g., come ~!)	hit	['hit]
there (e.g., to go ~)	dit	['dit]
from here (adv)	herfra	['hɛr,fra]
from there (adv)	derfra	['dɛr,fra]
close (adv)	nær	['nær]
far (adv)	langt	['laŋt]
near (e.g., ~ Paris)	nær	['nær]
nearby (adv)	i nærheten	[i 'nær,hetən]
not far (adv)	ikke langt	['ikə 'laŋt]
left (adj)	venstre	['vɛnstrə]
on the left	til venstre	[til 'vɛnstrə]
to the left	til venstre	[til 'vɛnstrə]
right (adj)	høyre	['højrə]
on the right	til høyre	[til 'højrə]
to the right	til høyre	[til 'højrə]
in front (adv)	foran	['fɔran]
front (as adj)	fremre	['frɛmrə]
ahead (the kids ran ~)	fram	['fram]
behind (adv)	bakom	['bakɔm]
from behind	bakfra	['bak,fra]

back (towards the rear)	tilbake	[til'bakə]
middle	midt (m)	['mit]
in the middle	i midten	[i 'mitən]

at the side	fra siden	[fra 'sidən]
everywhere (adv)	overalt	[ɔvər'alt]
around (in all directions)	rundt omkring	['rʉnt ɔm'kriŋ]

from inside	innefra	['inə‚fra]
somewhere (to go)	et sted	[et 'sted]
straight (directly)	rett, direkte	['rɛt], ['di'rɛktə]
back (e.g., come ~)	tilbake	[til'bakə]

| from anywhere | et eller annet steds fra | [et 'elər ‚a:nt 'stɛts fra] |
| from somewhere | et eller annet steds fra | [et 'elər ‚a:nt 'stɛts fra] |

firstly (adv)	for det første	[for de 'fœştə]
secondly (adv)	for det annet	[for de 'a:nt]
thirdly (adv)	for det tredje	[for de 'trɛdje]

suddenly (adv)	plutselig	['plʉtseli]
at first (in the beginning)	i begynnelsen	[i be'jinəlsən]
for the first time	for første gang	[for 'fœştə ‚gaŋ]
long before ...	lenge før ...	['leŋə 'før ...]
anew (over again)	på nytt	[pɔ 'nʏt]
for good (adv)	for godt	[for 'gɔt]

never (adv)	aldri	['aldri]
again (adv)	igjen	[i'jɛn]
now (adv)	nå	['nɔ]
often (adv)	ofte	['ɔftə]
then (adv)	da	['da]
urgently (quickly)	omgående	['ɔm‚gɔ:nə]
usually (adv)	vanligvis	['vanli‚vis]

by the way, ...	forresten, ...	[fɔ'rɛstən ...]
possible (that is ~)	mulig, kanskje	['mʉli], ['kanşə]
probably (adv)	sannsynligvis	[san'sʏnli‚vis]
maybe (adv)	kanskje	['kanşə]
besides ...	dessuten, ...	[des'ʉtən ...]
that's why ...	derfor ...	['dɛrfor ...]
in spite of ...	på tross av ...	['pɔ 'trɔs a: ...]
thanks to ...	takket være ...	['takət ‚værə ...]

what (pron.)	hva	['va]
that (conj.)	at	[at]
something	noe	['nʉe]
anything (something)	noe	['nʉe]
nothing	ingenting	['iŋəntiŋ]

| who (pron.) | hvem | ['vɛm] |
| someone | noen | ['nʉən] |

somebody	noen	['nʊən]
nobody	ingen	['iŋən]
nowhere (a voyage to ~)	ingensteds	['iŋən‚stɛts]
nobody's	ingens	['iŋəns]
somebody's	noens	['nʊəns]

so (I'm ~ glad)	så	['sɔ:]
also (as well)	også	['ɔsɔ]
too (as well)	også	['ɔsɔ]

6. Function words. Adverbs. Part 2

Why?	Hvorfor?	['vʊrfʊr]
for some reason	av en eller annen grunn	[ɑ: en elər 'ɑnən ‚grʊn]
because ...	fordi ,,,	[fɔ'di ...]
for some purpose	av en eller annen grunn	[ɑ: en elər 'ɑnən ‚grʊn]

and	og	['ɔ]
or	eller	['elər]
but	men	['men]
for (e.g., ~ me)	for, til	[fɔr], [til]

too (~ many people)	for, altfor	['fɔr], ['altfɔr]
only (exclusively)	bare	['bɑrə]
exactly (adv)	presis, eksakt	[prɛ'sis], [ɛk'sɑkt]
about (more or less)	cirka	['sirkɑ]

approximately (adv)	omtrent	[ɔm'trɛnt]
approximate (adj)	omtrentlig	[ɔm'trɛntli]
almost (adv)	nesten	['nɛstən]
the rest	rest (m)	['rɛst]

the other (second)	den annen	[den 'ɑnən]
other (different)	andre	['ɑndrə]
each (adj)	hver	['vɛr]
any (no matter which)	hvilken som helst	['vilkən sɔm 'hɛlst]
many, much (a lot of)	mye	['mye]
many people	mange	['mɑŋə]
all (everyone)	alle	['ɑlə]

in return for ...	til gjengjeld for ...	[til 'jɛnjɛl for ...]
in exchange (adv)	istedenfor	[i'stedən‚fɔr]
by hand (made)	for hånd	[fɔr 'hɔn]
hardly (negative opinion)	neppe	['nepə]

probably (adv)	sannsynligvis	[sɑn'sʏnli‚vis]
on purpose (intentionally)	med vilje	[me 'viljə]
by accident (adv)	tilfeldigvis	[til'fɛldivis]
very (adv)	meget	['megət]
for example (adv)	for eksempel	[fɔr ɛk'sɛmpəl]

between	**mellom**	['mɛlɔm]
among	**blant**	['blɑnt]
so much (such a lot)	**så mye**	['sɔː mye]
especially (adv)	**særlig**	['sæːli̩]

NUMBERS. MISCELLANEOUS

7. Cardinal numbers. Part 1

0 zero	null	['nʉl]
1 one	en	['en]
2 two	to	['tʊ]
3 three	tre	['tre]
4 four	fire	['fire]
5 five	fem	['fɛm]
6 six	seks	['sɛks]
7 seven	sju	['ʂʉ]
8 eight	åtte	['ɔtə]
9 nine	ni	['ni]
10 ten	ti	['ti]
11 eleven	elleve	['ɛlvə]
12 twelve	tolv	['tɔl]
13 thirteen	tretten	['trɛtən]
14 fourteen	fjorten	['fjɔ:ʈən]
15 fifteen	femten	['fɛmtən]
16 sixteen	seksten	['sæjstən]
17 seventeen	sytten	['sʏtən]
18 eighteen	atten	['atən]
19 nineteen	nitten	['nitən]
20 twenty	tjue	['çʉe]
21 twenty-one	tjueen	['çʉe en]
22 twenty-two	tjueto	['çʉe tʊ]
23 twenty-three	tjuetre	['çʉe tre]
30 thirty	tretti	['trɛti]
31 thirty-one	trettien	['trɛti en]
32 thirty-two	trettito	['trɛti tʊ]
33 thirty-three	trettitre	['trɛti tre]
40 forty	førti	['fœ:ʈi]
41 forty-one	førtien	['fœ:ʈi en]
42 forty-two	førtito	['fœ:ʈi tʊ]
43 forty-three	førtitre	['fœ:ʈi tre]
50 fifty	femti	['fɛmti]
51 fifty-one	femtien	['fɛmti en]
52 fifty-two	femtito	['fɛmti tʊ]

53 fifty-three	femtitre	['fɛmti tre]
60 sixty	seksti	['sɛksti]
61 sixty-one	sekstien	['sɛksti en]
62 sixty-two	sekstito	['sɛksti tʊ]
63 sixty-three	sekstitre	['sɛksti tre]

70 seventy	sytti	['sʏti]
71 seventy-one	syttien	['sʏti en]
72 seventy-two	syttito	['sʏti tʊ]
73 seventy-three	syttitre	['sʏti tre]

80 eighty	åtti	['ɔti]
81 eighty-one	åttien	['ɔti en]
82 eighty-two	åttito	['ɔti tʊ]
83 eighty-three	åttitre	['ɔti tre]

90 ninety	nitti	['niti]
91 ninety-one	nittien	['niti en]
92 ninety-two	nittito	['niti tʊ]
93 ninety-three	nittitre	['niti tre]

8. Cardinal numbers. Part 2

100 one hundred	hundre	['hʉndrə]
200 two hundred	to hundre	['tʊ ˌhʉndrə]
300 three hundred	tre hundre	['tre ˌhʉndrə]
400 four hundred	fire hundre	['fire ˌhʉndrə]
500 five hundred	fem hundre	['fɛm ˌhʉndrə]

600 six hundred	seks hundre	['sɛks ˌhʉndrə]
700 seven hundred	syv hundre	['syv ˌhʉndrə]
800 eight hundred	åtte hundre	['ɔtə ˌhʉndrə]
900 nine hundred	ni hundre	['ni ˌhʉndrə]

1000 one thousand	tusen	['tʉsən]
2000 two thousand	to tusen	['tʊ ˌtʉsən]
3000 three thousand	tre tusen	['tre ˌtʉsən]
10000 ten thousand	ti tusen	['ti ˌtʉsən]
one hundred thousand	hundre tusen	['hʉndrə ˌtʉsən]
million	million (m)	[mi'ljun]
billion	milliard (m)	[mi'lja:ɖ]

9. Ordinal numbers

first (adj)	første	['fœʂtə]
second (adj)	annen	['ɑnən]
third (adj)	tredje	['trɛdjə]
fourth (adj)	fjerde	['fjærə]

fifth (adj)	**femte**	[ˈfɛmtə]
sixth (adj)	**sjette**	[ˈʂɛtə]
seventh (adj)	**sjuende**	[ˈʂʉenə]
eighth (adj)	**åttende**	[ˈɔtenə]
ninth (adj)	**niende**	[ˈnienə]
tenth (adj)	**tiende**	[ˈtienə]

COLOURS. UNITS OF MEASUREMENT

10. Colors

color	farge (m)	['fɑrgə]
shade (tint)	nyanse (m)	[ny'ɑnse]
hue	fargetone (m)	['fɑrgə,tʊnə]
rainbow	regnbue (m)	['ræjn,bʉːə]
white (adj)	hvit	['vit]
black (adj)	svart	['svɑːt]
gray (adj)	grå	['grɔ]
green (adj)	grønn	['grœn]
yellow (adj)	gul	['gʉl]
red (adj)	rød	['rø]
blue (adj)	blå	['blɔ]
light blue (adj)	lyseblå	['lysə,blɔ]
pink (adj)	rosa	['rosɑ]
orange (adj)	oransje	[ɔ'rɑnʂɛ]
violet (adj)	fiolett	[fiʊ'lət]
brown (adj)	brun	['brʉn]
golden (adj)	gullgul	['gʉl]
silvery (adj)	sølv-	['søl-]
beige (adj)	beige	['bɛːʂ]
cream (adj)	kremfarget	['krɛm,fɑrgət]
turquoise (adj)	turkis	[tʉr'kis]
cherry red (adj)	kirsebærrød	['çiʂəbær,rød]
lilac (adj)	lilla	['lilɑ]
crimson (adj)	karminrød	['kɑrmʊ'sin,rød]
light (adj)	lys	['lys]
dark (adj)	mørk	['mœrk]
bright, vivid (adj)	klar	['klɑr]
colored (pencils)	farge-	['fɑrgə-]
color (e.g., ~ film)	farge-	['fɑrgə-]
black-and-white (adj)	svart-hvit	['svɑːt vit]
plain (one-colored)	ensfarget	['ɛns,fɑrgət]
multicolored (adj)	mangefarget	['mɑŋə,fɑrgət]

11. Units of measurement

weight	vekt (m)	['vɛkt]
length	lengde (m/f)	['leŋdə]
width	bredde (m)	['brɛdə]
height	høyde (m)	['højdə]
depth	dybde (m)	['dʏbdə]
volume	volum (n)	[vɔ'lʉm]
area	areal (n)	[ˌare'al]

gram	gram (n)	['gram]
milligram	milligram (n)	['miliˌgram]
kilogram	kilogram (n)	['çiluˌgram]
ton	tonn (m/n)	['tɔn]
pound	pund (n)	['pʉn]
ounce	unse (m)	['ʉnsə]

meter	meter (m)	['metər]
millimeter	millimeter (m)	['miliˌmetər]
centimeter	centimeter (m)	['sɛntiˌmetər]
kilometer	kilometer (m)	['çiluˌmetər]
mile	mil (m/f)	['mil]

inch	tomme (m)	['tɔmə]
foot	fot (m)	['fʊt]
yard	yard (m)	['jaːrd]

| square meter | kvadratmeter (m) | [kva'dratˌmetər] |
| hectare | hektar (n) | ['hɛktar] |

liter	liter (m)	['litər]
degree	grad (m)	['grad]
volt	volt (m)	['vɔlt]
ampere	ampere (m)	[am'pɛr]
horsepower	hestekraft (m/f)	['hɛstəˌkraft]

quantity	mengde (m)	['mɛŋdə]
a little bit of ...	få ...	['fɔ ...]
half	halvdel (m)	['haldel]

| dozen | dusin (n) | [dʉ'sin] |
| piece (item) | stykke (n) | ['stʏkə] |

| size | størrelse (m) | ['stœrəlsə] |
| scale (map ~) | målestokk (m) | ['moːləˌstɔk] |

minimal (adj)	minimal	[mini'mal]
the smallest (adj)	minste	['minstə]
medium (adj)	middel-	['midəl-]
maximal (adj)	maksimal	[maksi'mal]
the largest (adj)	største	['stœʂtə]

12. Containers

canning jar (glass ~)	glaskrukke (m/f)	['glas,krʉkə]
can	boks (m)	['bɔks]
bucket	bøtte (m/f)	['bœtə]
barrel	tønne (m)	['tœnə]

wash basin (e.g., plastic ~)	vaskefat (n)	['vaskə,fat]
tank (100L water ~)	tank (m)	['taŋk]
hip flask	lommelerke (m/f)	['lʊmə,lærkə]
jerrycan	bensinkanne (m/f)	[bɛn'sin,kanə]
tank (e.g., tank car)	tank (m)	['taŋk]

mug	krus (n)	['krʉs]
cup (of coffee, etc.)	kopp (m)	['kɔp]
saucer	tefat (n)	['te,fat]
glass (tumbler)	glass (n)	['glas]
wine glass	vinglass (n)	['vin,glas]
stock pot (soup pot)	gryte (m/f)	['grytə]

bottle (~ of wine)	flaske (m)	['flaskə]
neck (of the bottle, etc.)	flaskehals (m)	['flaskə,hals]

carafe (decanter)	karaffel (m)	[ka'rafəl]
pitcher	mugge (m/f)	['mʉgə]
vessel (container)	beholder (m)	[be'hɔlər]
pot (crock, stoneware ~)	pott, potte (m)	['pɔt], ['pɔtə]
vase	vase (m)	['vasə]

bottle (perfume ~)	flakong (m)	[fla'kɔŋ]
vial, small bottle	flaske (m/f)	['flaskə]
tube (of toothpaste)	tube (m)	['tʉbə]

sack (bag)	sekk (m)	['sɛk]
bag (paper ~, plastic ~)	pose (m)	['pʊsə]
pack (of cigarettes, etc.)	pakke (m/f)	['pakə]

box (e.g., shoebox)	eske (m/f)	['ɛskə]
crate	kasse (m/f)	['kasə]
basket	kurv (m)	['kʉrv]

MAIN VERBS

13. The most important verbs. Part 1

to advise (vt)	å råde	[ɔ 'roːdə]
to agree (say yes)	å samtykke	[ɔ 'samˌtʏkə]
to answer (vi, vt)	å svare	[ɔ 'svarə]
to apologize (vi)	å unnskylde seg	[ɔ 'ʉnˌʂylə sæj]
to arrive (vi)	å ankomme	[ɔ 'anˌkɔmə]
to ask (~ oneself)	å spørre	[ɔ 'spørə]
to ask (~ sb to do sth)	å be	[ɔ 'be]
to be (vi)	å være	[ɔ 'væɾə]
to be afraid	å frykte	[ɔ 'frʏktə]
to be hungry	å være sulten	[ɔ 'væɾə 'sʉltən]
to be interested in ...	å interessere seg	[ɔ intəre'serə sæj]
to be needed	å være behøv	[ɔ 'væɾə bə'høv]
to be surprised	å bli forundret	[ɔ 'bli fɔ'ɾʉndrət]
to be thirsty	å være tørst	[ɔ 'væɾə 'tœʂt]
to begin (vt)	å begynne	[ɔ be'jinə]
to belong to ...	å tilhøre ...	[ɔ 'tilˌhøɾə ...]
to boast (vi)	å prale	[ɔ 'pralə]
to break (split into pieces)	å bryte	[ɔ 'brytə]
to call (~ for help)	å tilkalle	[ɔ 'tilˌkalə]
can (v aux)	å kunne	[ɔ 'kʉnə]
to catch (vt)	å fange	[ɔ 'faŋə]
to change (vt)	å endre	[ɔ 'ɛndrə]
to choose (select)	å velge	[ɔ 'vɛlgə]
to come down (the stairs)	å gå ned	[ɔ 'gɔ ne]
to compare (vt)	å sammenlikne	[ɔ 'samənˌliknə]
to complain (vi, vt)	å klage	[ɔ 'klagə]
to confuse (mix up)	å forveksle	[ɔ fɔr'vɛkʂlə]
to continue (vt)	å fortsette	[ɔ 'fɔrtˌsɛtə]
to control (vt)	å kontrollere	[ɔ kʉntrɔ'lerə]
to cook (dinner)	å lage	[ɔ 'lagə]
to cost (vt)	å koste	[ɔ 'kɔstə]
to count (add up)	å telle	[ɔ 'tɛlə]
to count on ...	å regne med ...	[ɔ 'rɛjnə me ...]
to create (vt)	å opprette	[ɔ 'ɔpˌrɛtə]
to cry (weep)	å gråte	[ɔ 'groːtə]

14. The most important verbs. Part 2

to deceive (vi, vt)	å fuske	[ɔ 'fʉskə]
to decorate (tree, street)	å pryde	[ɔ 'prydə]
to defend (a country, etc.)	å forsvare	[ɔ fɔ'ʂvɑrə]
to demand (request firmly)	å kreve	[ɔ 'krevə]
to dig (vt)	å grave	[ɔ 'grɑvə]
to discuss (vt)	å diskutere	[ɔ diskʉ'terə]
to do (vt)	å gjøre	[ɔ 'jørə]
to doubt (have doubts)	å tvile	[ɔ 'tvilə]
to drop (let fall)	å tappe	[ɔ 'tɑpə]
to enter (room, house, etc.)	å komme inn	[ɔ 'kɔmə in]
to excuse (forgive)	å unnskylde	[ɔ 'ʉn‚ʂylə]
to exist (vi)	å eksistere	[ɔ ɛksi'sterə]
to expect (foresee)	å forutse	[ɔ 'forʉt‚se]
to explain (vt)	å forklare	[ɔ fɔr'klɑrə]
to fall (vi)	å falle	[ɔ 'fɑlə]
to find (vt)	å finne	[ɔ 'finə]
to finish (vt)	å slutte	[ɔ 'ʂlʉtə]
to fly (vi)	å fly	[ɔ 'fly]
to follow ... (come after)	å følge etter ...	[ɔ 'følə 'ɛtər ...]
to forget (vi, vt)	å glemme	[ɔ 'glemə]
to forgive (vt)	å tilgi	[ɔ 'til‚ji]
to give (vt)	å gi	[ɔ 'ji]
to give a hint	å gi et vink	[ɔ 'ji et 'vink]
to go (on foot)	å gå	[ɔ 'gɔ]
to go for a swim	å bade	[ɔ 'bɑdə]
to go out (for dinner, etc.)	å gå ut	[ɔ 'gɔ ʉt]
to guess (the answer)	å gjette	[ɔ 'jɛtə]
to have (vt)	å ha	[ɔ 'hɑ]
to have breakfast	å spise frokost	[ɔ 'spisə ‚frʉkɔst]
to have dinner	å spise middag	[ɔ 'spisə 'mi‚dɑ]
to have lunch	å spise lunsj	[ɔ 'spisə ‚lʉnʂ]
to hear (vt)	å høre	[ɔ 'hørə]
to help (vt)	å hjelpe	[ɔ 'jɛlpə]
to hide (vt)	å gjemme	[ɔ 'jɛmə]
to hope (vi, vt)	å håpe	[ɔ 'hoːpə]
to hunt (vi, vt)	å jage	[ɔ 'jɑgə]
to hurry (vi)	å skynde seg	[ɔ 'ʂynə sæj]

15. The most important verbs. Part 3

to inform (vt)	å informere	[ɔ infɔr'merə]
to insist (vi, vt)	å insistere	[ɔ insi'sterə]
to insult (vt)	å fornærme	[ɔ fɔː'nærmə]
to invite (vt)	å innby, å invitere	[ɔ 'inby], [ɔ invi'terə]
to joke (vi)	å spøke	[ɔ 'spøkə]
to keep (vt)	å beholde	[ɔ be'hɔlə]
to keep silent	å tie	[ɔ 'tie]
to kill (vt)	å døde, å myrde	[ɔ 'dødə], [ɔ 'mʏːdə]
to know (sb)	å kjenne	[ɔ 'çɛnə]
to know (sth)	å vite	[ɔ 'vitə]
to laugh (vi)	å le, å skratte	[ɔ 'le], [ɔ 'skrɑtə]
to liberate (city, etc.)	å befri	[ɔ be'fri]
to like (I like ...)	å like	[ɔ 'likə]
to look for ... (search)	å søke ...	[ɔ 'søkə ...]
to love (sb)	å elske	[ɔ 'ɛlskə]
to make a mistake	å gjøre feil	[ɔ 'jørə ˌfæjl]
to manage, to run	å styre, å lede	[ɔ 'styrə], [ɔ 'ledə]
to mean (signify)	å bety	[ɔ 'bety]
to mention (talk about)	å omtale, å nevne	[ɔ 'ɔmˌtɑlə], [ɔ 'nɛvnə]
to miss (school, etc.)	å skulke	[ɔ 'skʉlkə]
to notice (see)	å bemerke	[ɔ be'mærkə]
to object (vi, vt)	å innvende	[ɔ 'inˌvɛnə]
to observe (see)	å observere	[ɔ ɔbsɛr'verə]
to open (vt)	å åpne	[ɔ 'ɔpnə]
to order (meal, etc.)	å bestille	[ɔ be'stilə]
to order (mil.)	å beordre	[ɔ be'ɔrdrə]
to own (possess)	å besidde, å eie	[ɔ bɛ'sidə], [ɔ 'æje]
to participate (vi)	å delta	[ɔ 'dɛltɑ]
to pay (vi, vt)	å betale	[ɔ be'tɑlə]
to permit (vt)	å tillate	[ɔ 'tiˌlɑtə]
to plan (vt)	å planlegge	[ɔ 'plɑnˌlegə]
to play (children)	å leke	[ɔ 'lekə]
to pray (vi, vt)	å be	[ɔ 'be]
to prefer (vt)	å foretrekke	[ɔ 'fɔrəˌtrɛkə]
to promise (vt)	å love	[ɔ 'lɔvə]
to pronounce (vt)	å uttale	[ɔ 'ʉtˌtɑlə]
to propose (vt)	å foreslå	[ɔ 'fɔrəˌslɔ]
to punish (vt)	å straffe	[ɔ 'strɑfə]

16. The most important verbs. Part 4

to read (vi, vt)	å lese	[ɔ 'lesə]
to recommend (vt)	å anbefale	[ɔ 'ɑnbeˌfɑlə]

to refuse (vi, vt)	å vegre seg	[ɔ 'vɛgrə sæj]
to regret (be sorry)	å beklage	[ɔ be'klɑgə]
to rent (sth from sb)	å leie	[ɔ 'læjə]
to repeat (say again)	å gjenta	[ɔ 'jɛntɑ]
to reserve, to book	å reservere	[ɔ resɛr'verə]
to run (vi)	å løpe	[ɔ 'løpə]
to save (rescue)	å redde	[ɔ 'rɛdə]
to say (~ thank you)	å si	[ɔ 'si]
to scold (vt)	å skjelle	[ɔ 'ʂɛːlə]
to see (vt)	å se	[ɔ 'se]
to sell (vt)	å selge	[ɔ 'sɛlə]
to send (vt)	å sende	[ɔ 'sɛnə]
to shoot (vi)	å skyte	[ɔ 'ʂytə]
to shout (vi)	å skrike	[ɔ 'skrikə]
to show (vt)	å vise	[ɔ 'visə]
to sign (document)	å underskrive	[ɔ 'unə͵skrivə]
to sit down (vi)	å sette seg	[ɔ 'sɛtə sæj]
to smile (vi)	å smile	[ɔ 'smilə]
to speak (vi, vt)	å tale	[ɔ 'tɑlə]
to steal (money, etc.)	å stjele	[ɔ 'stjelə]
to stop (for pause, etc.)	å stoppe	[ɔ 'stɔpə]
to stop (please ~ calling me)	å slutte	[ɔ 'ʂlʉtə]
to study (vt)	å studere	[ɔ stʉ'derə]
to swim (vi)	å svømme	[ɔ 'svœmə]
to take (vt)	å ta	[ɔ 'tɑ]
to think (vi, vt)	å tenke	[ɔ 'tɛnkə]
to threaten (vt)	å true	[ɔ 'trʉə]
to touch (with hands)	å røre	[ɔ 'rørə]
to translate (vt)	å oversette	[ɔ 'ɔvə͵sɛtə]
to trust (vt)	å stole på	[ɔ 'stʉlə pɔ]
to try (attempt)	å prøve	[ɔ 'prøvə]
to turn (e.g., ~ left)	å svinge	[ɔ 'sviŋə]
to underestimate (vt)	å undervurdere	[ɔ 'ʉnərvʉː͵derə]
to understand (vt)	å forstå	[ɔ fɔ'ʂtɔ]
to unite (vt)	å forene	[ɔ fɔ'renə]
to wait (vt)	å vente	[ɔ 'vɛntə]
to want (wish, desire)	å ville	[ɔ 'vilə]
to warn (vt)	å varsle	[ɔ 'vɑʂlə]
to work (vi)	å arbeide	[ɔ 'ɑr͵bæjdə]
to write (vt)	å skrive	[ɔ 'skrivə]
to write down	å skrive ned	[ɔ 'skrivə ne]

TIME. CALENDAR

17. Weekdays

Monday	mandag (m)	['manˌdɑ]
Tuesday	tirsdag (m)	['tiʂˌdɑ]
Wednesday	onsdag (m)	['ʊnsˌdɑ]
Thursday	torsdag (m)	['tɔʂˌdɑ]
Friday	fredag (m)	['frɛˌdɑ]
Saturday	lørdag (m)	['løɾˌdɑ]
Sunday	søndag (m)	['sønˌdɑ]

today (adv)	i dag	[i 'dɑ]
tomorrow (adv)	i morgen	[i 'mɔːən]
the day after tomorrow	i overmorgen	[i 'ɔvəɾˌmɔːən]
yesterday (adv)	i går	[i 'gɔr]
the day before yesterday	i forgårs	[i 'fɔɾˌgɔʂ]

day	dag (m)	['dɑ]
working day	arbeidsdag (m)	['ɑrbæjdsˌdɑ]
public holiday	festdag (m)	['fɛstˌdɑ]
day off	fridag (m)	['friˌdɑ]
weekend	ukeslutt (m), helg (f)	['ʉkəˌslʉt], ['hɛlg]

all day long	hele dagen	['helə 'dɑgən]
the next day (adv)	neste dag	['nɛstə ˌdɑ]
two days ago	for to dager siden	[fɔr tʊ 'dɑgər ˌsidən]
the day before	dagen før	['dɑgən 'før]
daily (adj)	daglig	['dɑgli]
every day (adv)	hver dag	['vɛr dɑ]

week	uke (m/f)	['ʉkə]
last week (adv)	siste uke	['sistə 'ʉkə]
next week (adv)	i neste uke	[i 'nɛstə 'ʉkə]
weekly (adj)	ukentlig	['ʉkəntli]
every week (adv)	hver uke	['vɛr 'ʉkə]
twice a week	to ganger per uke	['tʊ 'gaŋər per 'ʉkə]
every Tuesday	hver tirsdag	['vɛr 'tiʂdɑ]

18. Hours. Day and night

morning	morgen (m)	['mɔːən]
in the morning	om morgenen	[ɔm 'mɔːenən]
noon, midday	middag (m)	['miˌdɑ]

in the afternoon	om ettermiddagen	[ɔm 'ɛtərˌmidɑgən]
evening	kveld (m)	['kvɛl]
in the evening	om kvelden	[ɔm 'kvɛlən]
night	natt (m/f)	['nɑt]
at night	om natta	[ɔm 'nɑtɑ]
midnight	midnatt (m/f)	['midˌnɑt]

second	sekund (m/n)	[se'kʉn]
minute	minutt (n)	[mi'nʉt]
hour	time (m)	['timə]
half an hour	halvtime (m)	['hɑlˌtimə]
a quarter-hour	kvarter (n)	[kvɑːʈer]
fifteen minutes	femten minutter	['fɛmtən mi'nʉtər]
24 hours	døgn (n)	['døjn]

sunrise	soloppgang (m)	['sʉlɔpˌgɑŋ]
dawn	daggry (n)	['dɑgˌgry]
early morning	tidlig morgen (m)	['tili 'mɔːən]
sunset	solnedgang (m)	['sʉlnedˌgɑŋ]

early in the morning	tidlig om morgenen	['tili ɔm 'mɔːenen]
this morning	i morges	[i 'mɔrəs]
tomorrow morning	i morgen tidlig	[i 'mɔːən 'tili]

this afternoon	i formiddag	[i 'fɔrmiˌdɑ]
in the afternoon	om ettermiddagen	[ɔm 'ɛtərˌmidɑgən]
tomorrow afternoon	i morgen ettermiddag	[i 'mɔːən 'ɛtərˌmidɑ]

| tonight (this evening) | i kveld | [i 'kvɛl] |
| tomorrow night | i morgen kveld | [i 'mɔːən ˌkvɛl] |

at 3 o'clock sharp	presis klokka tre	[prɛ'sis 'klɔkɑ tre]
about 4 o'clock	ved fire-tiden	[ve 'fire ˌtidən]
by 12 o'clock	innen klokken tolv	['inən 'klɔkən tɔl]

in 20 minutes	om tjue minutter	[ɔm 'çʉə mi'nʉtər]
in an hour	om en time	[ɔm en 'timə]
on time (adv)	i tide	[i 'tidə]

a quarter of …	kvart på …	['kvɑːʈ pɔ …]
within an hour	innen en time	['inən en 'timə]
every 15 minutes	hvert kvarter	['vɛːʈ kvɑ:'ʈer]
round the clock	døgnet rundt	['døjne ˌrʉnt]

19. Months. Seasons

January	januar (m)	['jɑnʉˌɑr]
February	februar (m)	['febrʉˌɑr]
March	mars (m)	['mɑʂ]
April	april (m)	[ɑ'pril]

May	mai (m)	['mɑj]
June	juni (m)	['jʉni]

July	juli (m)	['jʉli]
August	august (m)	[aʉ'gʉst]
September	september (m)	[sep'tɛmbər]
October	oktober (m)	[ɔk'tʉbər]
November	november (m)	[nʉ'vɛmbər]
December	desember (m)	[de'sɛmbər]

spring	vår (m)	['vɔːr]
in spring	om våren	[ɔm 'vɔːrən]
spring (as adj)	vår-, vårlig	['vɔːr-], ['vɔːli]

summer	sommer (m)	['sɔmər]
in summer	om sommeren	[ɔm 'sɔmerən]
summer (as adj)	sommer-	['sɔmər-]

fall	høst (m)	['høst]
in fall	om høsten	[ɔm 'høstən]
fall (as adj)	høst-, høstlig	['høst-], ['høstli]

winter	vinter (m)	['vintər]
in winter	om vinteren	[ɔm 'vinterən]
winter (as adj)	vinter-	['vintər-]

month	måned (m)	['moːnət]
this month	denne måneden	['dɛnə 'moːnedən]
next month	neste måned	['nɛstə 'moːnət]
last month	forrige måned	['fɔriə ˌmoːnət]

a month ago	for en måned siden	[fɔr en 'moːnət ˌsidən]
in a month (a month later)	om en måned	[ɔm en 'moːnət]
in 2 months (2 months later)	om to måneder	[ɔm 'tʉ 'moːnedər]
the whole month	en hel måned	[en 'hel 'moːnət]
all month long	hele måned	['helə 'moːnət]

monthly (~ magazine)	månedlig	['moːnədli]
monthly (adv)	månedligt	['moːnedlət]
every month	hver måned	[ˌvɛr 'moːnət]
twice a month	to ganger per måned	['tʉ 'gɑŋər per 'moːnət]

year	år (n)	['ɔr]
this year	i år	[i 'oːr]
next year	neste år	['nɛstə ˌoːr]
last year	i fjor	[i 'fjɔr]

a year ago	for et år siden	[fɔr et 'oːr ˌsidən]
in a year	om et år	[ɔm et 'oːr]
in two years	om to år	[ɔm 'tʉ 'oːr]
the whole year	hele året	['helə 'oːre]

all year long	hele året	['helə 'oːre]
every year	hvert år	['vɛːʈ 'oːr]
annual (adj)	årlig	['oːli]
annually (adv)	årlig, hvert år	['oːli], ['vɛːʈ 'ɔr]
4 times a year	fire ganger per år	['fire 'gaŋər per 'oːr]

date (e.g., today's ~)	dato (m)	['dɑtʊ]
date (e.g., ~ of birth)	dato (m)	['dɑtʊ]
calendar	kalender (m)	[kɑ'lendər]

half a year	halvår (n)	['hɑl‚oːr]
six months	halvår (n)	['hɑl‚oːr]
season (summer, etc.)	årstid (m/f)	['oːs‚tid]
century	århundre (n)	['ɔr‚hʊndrə]

TRAVEL. HOTEL

20. Trip. Travel

tourism, travel	turisme (m)	[tʉˈrismə]
tourist	turist (m)	[tʉˈrist]
trip, voyage	reise (m/f)	[ˈræjsə]
adventure	eventyr (n)	[ˈɛvənˌtyr]
trip, journey	tripp (m)	[ˈtrip]
vacation	ferie (m)	[ˈfɛriə]
to be on vacation	å være på ferie	[ɔ ˈværə pɔ ˈfɛriə]
rest	hvile (m/f)	[ˈvilə]
train	tog (n)	[ˈtɔg]
by train	med tog	[me ˈtɔg]
airplane	fly (n)	[ˈfly]
by airplane	med fly	[me ˈfly]
by car	med bil	[me ˈbil]
by ship	med skip	[me ˈʂip]
luggage	bagasje (m)	[bɑˈgɑʂə]
suitcase	koffert (m)	[ˈkʊfɛːt]
luggage cart	bagasjetralle (m/f)	[bɑˈgɑʂəˌtrɑlə]
passport	pass (n)	[ˈpɑs]
visa	visum (n)	[ˈvisʉm]
ticket	billett (m)	[biˈlet]
air ticket	flybillett (m)	[ˈfly biˈlet]
guidebook	reisehåndbok (m/f)	[ˈræjsəˌhɔnbʊk]
map (tourist ~)	kart (n)	[ˈkɑːt]
area (rural ~)	område (n)	[ˈɔmˌroːdə]
place, site	sted (n)	[ˈsted]
exotic (adj)	eksotisk	[ɛkˈsʊtisk]
amazing (adj)	forunderlig	[fɔˈrʉndeːli]
group	gruppe (m)	[ˈgrʉpə]
excursion, sightseeing tour	utflukt (m/f)	[ˈʉtˌflʉkt]
guide (person)	guide (m)	[ˈgɑjd]

21. Hotel

hotel	hotell (n)	[hʊˈtɛl]
motel	motell (n)	[mʊˈtɛl]

three-star (~ hotel)	trestjernet	['tre.stjæ:ŋə]
five-star	femstjernet	['fɛm.stjæ:ŋə]
to stay (in a hotel, etc.)	å bo	[ɔ 'buʹ]

room	rom (n)	['rʊm]
single room	enkeltrom (n)	['ɛnkelt.rʊm]
double room	dobbeltrom (n)	['dɔbəlt.rʊm]
to book a room	å reservere rom	[ɔ resɛr'verə 'rʊm]

half board	halvpensjon (m)	['hal pɑn.ʂʊn]
full board	fullpensjon (m)	['fʉl pɑn.ʂʊn]

with bath	med badekar	[me 'badə.kɑr]
with shower	med dusj	[me 'dʉʂ]
satellite television	satellitt-TV (m)	[sɑtɛ'lit 'tɛvɛ]
air-conditioner	klimaanlegg (n)	['klima'ɑn.leg]
towel	håndkle (n)	['hɔn.kle]
key	nøkkel (m)	['nøkəl]

administrator	administrator (m)	[admini'strɑ:tʊr]
chambermaid	stuepike (m/f)	['stʉə.pikə]
porter, bellboy	pikkolo (m)	['pikɔlɔ]
doorman	portier (m)	[pɔ:'tje]

restaurant	restaurant (m)	[rɛstʉ'rɑŋ]
pub, bar	bar (m)	['bɑr]
breakfast	frokost (m)	['frʊkɔst]
dinner	middag (m)	['mi.dɑ]
buffet	buffet (m)	[bʉ'fɛ]

lobby	hall, lobby (m)	['hal], ['lɔbi]
elevator	heis (m)	['hæjs]

DO NOT DISTURB	VENNLIGST IKKE FORSTYRR!	['vɛnligt ikə fɔ'ʂtyr]
NO SMOKING	RØYKING FORBUDT	['røjkiŋ fɔr'bʉt]

22. Sightseeing

monument	monument (n)	[mɔnʉ'mɛnt]
fortress	festning (m/f)	['fɛstniŋ]
palace	palass (n)	[pɑ'las]
castle	borg (m)	['bɔrg]
tower	tårn (n)	['tɔ:ŋ]
mausoleum	mausoleum (n)	[mɑʊsʊ'leum]

architecture	arkitektur (m)	[ɑrkitɛk'tʉr]
medieval (adj)	middelalderlig	['midəl.ɑldɛ:[i]
ancient (adj)	gammel	['gaməl]
national (adj)	nasjonal	[naʂʊ'nal]

famous (monument, etc.)	**kjent**	['çɛnt]
tourist	**turist** (m)	[tʉ'rist]
guide (person)	**guide** (m)	['gɑjd]
excursion, sightseeing tour	**utflukt** (m/f)	['ʉtˌflʉkt]
to show (vt)	**å vise**	[ɔ 'visə]
to tell (vt)	**å fortelle**	[ɔ fɔː'ʈɛlə]
to find (vt)	**å finne**	[ɔ 'finə]
to get lost (lose one's way)	**å gå seg bort**	[ɔ 'gɔ sæj 'bʉːʈ]
map (e.g., subway ~)	**kart, linjekart** (n)	['kɑːʈ], ['linjə'kɑːʈ]
map (e.g., city ~)	**kart** (n)	['kɑːʈ]
souvenir, gift	**suvenir** (m)	[sʉve'nir]
gift shop	**suvenirbutikk** (m)	[sʉve'nir bʉ'tik]
to take pictures	**å fotografere**	[ɔ fotɔgrɑ'ferə]
to have one's picture taken	**å bli fotografert**	[ɔ 'bli fotɔgrɑ'fɛːʈ]

TRANSPORTATION

23. Airport

airport	flyplass (m)	['fly,plɑs]
airplane	fly (n)	['fly]
airline	flyselskap (n)	['flysəl,skɑp]
air traffic controller	flygeleder (m)	['flygə,ledər]

departure	avgang (m)	['ɑv,gɑŋ]
arrival	ankomst (m)	['ɑn,kɔmst]
to arrive (by plane)	å ankomme	[ɔ 'ɑn,kɔmə]

departure time	avgangstid (m/f)	['ɑvgɑŋs,tid]
arrival time	ankomsttid (m/f)	[ɑn'kɔms,tid]

to be delayed	å bli forsinket	[ɔ 'bli fɔ'ʂinkət]
flight delay	avgangsforsinkelse (m)	['ɑvgɑŋs fɔ'ʂinkəlsə]

information board	informasjonstavle (m/f)	[infɔrmɑ'ʂʉns ,tɑvlə]
information	informasjon (m)	[infɔrmɑ'ʂʉn]
to announce (vt)	å meddele	[ɔ 'mɛd,delə]
flight (e.g., next ~)	fly (n)	['fly]

customs	toll (m)	['tɔl]
customs officer	tollbetjent (m)	['tɔlbe,tjɛnt]

customs declaration	tolldeklarasjon (m)	['tɔldɛklɑrɑ'ʂʉn]
to fill out (vt)	å utfylle	[ɔ 'ʉt,fʏlə]
to fill out the declaration	å utfylle en tolldeklarasjon	[ɔ 'ʉt,fʏlə en 'tɔldɛklɑrɑ,ʂʉn]
passport control	passkontroll (m)	['pɑskʉn,trɔl]

luggage	bagasje (m)	[bɑ'gɑʂə]
hand luggage	håndbagasje (m)	['hɔn,bɑ'gɑʂə]
luggage cart	bagasjetralle (m/f)	[bɑ'gɑʂə,trɑlə]

landing	landing (m)	['lɑniŋ]
landing strip	landingsbane (m)	['lɑniŋs,bɑnə]
to land (vi)	å lande	[ɔ 'lɑnə]
airstairs	trapp (m/f)	['trɑp]

check-in	innsjekking (m/f)	['in,ʂɛkiŋ]
check-in counter	innsjekkingsskranke (m)	['in,ʂɛkiŋs ,skrɑnkə]
to check-in (vi)	å sjekke inn	[ɔ 'ʂɛkə in]
boarding pass	boardingkort (n)	['bɔːdiŋ,kɔːt]

departure gate	gate (m/f)	['gejt]
transit	transitt (m)	[tran'sit]
to wait (vt)	å vente	[ɔ 'vɛntə]
departure lounge	ventehall (m)	['vɛntə‚hal]
to see off	å ta avskjed	[ɔ 'ta 'af‚sɛd]
to say goodbye	å si farvel	[ɔ 'si far'vɛl]

24. Airplane

airplane	fly (n)	['fly]
air ticket	flybillett (m)	['fly bi'let]
airline	flyselskap (n)	['flysəl‚skap]
airport	flyplass (m)	['fly‚plas]
supersonic (adj)	overlyds-	['ɔvə‚lyds-]

captain	kaptein (m)	[kap'tæjn]
crew	besetning (m/f)	[be'sɛtniŋ]
pilot	pilot (m)	[pi'lɔt]
flight attendant (fem.)	flyvertinne (m/f)	[flyvɛ:'t̪inə]
navigator	styrmann (m)	['styr‚man]

wings	vinger (m pl)	['viŋər]
tail	hale (m)	['halə]
cockpit	cockpit, førerkabin (m)	['kɔkpit], ['førərka‚bin]
engine	motor (m)	['mɔtʊr]
undercarriage (landing gear)	landingshjul (n)	['laniŋsjʉl]
turbine	turbin (m)	[tʉr'bin]

propeller	propell (m)	[prʊ'pɛl]
black box	svart boks (m)	['sva:t̪ bɔks]
yoke (control column)	ratt (n)	['rat]
fuel	brensel (n)	['brɛnsəl]

safety card	sikkerhetsbrosjyre (m)	['sikərhɛts‚brɔ'ʂyrə]
oxygen mask	oksygenmaske (m/f)	['ɔksygən‚maskə]
uniform	uniform (m)	[ʉni'fɔrm]
life vest	redningsvest (m)	['rɛdniŋs‚vɛst]
parachute	fallskjerm (m)	['fal‚ʂærm]

takeoff	start (m)	['sta:t̪]
to take off (vi)	å løfte	[ɔ 'lœftə]
runway	startbane (m)	['sta:t̪‚banə]

visibility	siktbarhet (m)	['siktbar‚het]
flight (act of flying)	flyging (m/f)	['flygiŋ]
altitude	høyde (m)	['højdə]
air pocket	lufthull (n)	['lʉft‚hʉl]
seat	plass (m)	['plas]
headphones	hodetelefoner (n pl)	['hɔdətelə‚fʊnər]

folding tray (tray table)	klappbord (n)	['klɑp,bʊr]
airplane window	vindu (n)	['vindʉ]
aisle	midtgang (m)	['mit,gɑŋ]

25. Train

train	tog (n)	['tɔg]
commuter train	lokaltog (n)	[lɔ'kɑl,tɔg]
express train	ekspresstog (n)	[ɛks'prɛs,tɔg]
diesel locomotive	diesellokomotiv (n)	['disəl lʊkɔmɔ'tiv]
steam locomotive	damplokomotiv (n)	['dɑmp lʊkɔmɔ'tiv]

| passenger car | vogn (m) | ['vɔŋn] |
| dining car | restaurantvogn (m/f) | [rɛstʊ'rɑŋ,vɔŋn] |

rails	skinner (m/f pl)	['ṣinər]
railroad	jernbane (m)	['jæː,n̩bɑne]
railway tie	sville (m/f)	['svilə]

platform (railway ~)	perrong, plattform (m/f)	[pɛ'rɔŋ], ['plɑtfɔrm]
track (~ 1, 2, etc.)	spor (n)	['spʊr]
semaphore	semafor (m)	[semɑ'fʊr]
station	stasjon (m)	[stɑ'ṣʊn]

engineer (train driver)	lokfører (m)	['lʊk,førər]
porter (of luggage)	bærer (m)	['bærər]
car attendant	betjent (m)	['be'tjɛnt]
passenger	passasjer (m)	[pɑsɑ'ṣɛr]
conductor (ticket inspector)	billett inspektør (m)	[bi'let inspɛk'tør]

| corridor (in train) | korridor (m) | [kʊri'dɔr] |
| emergency brake | nødbrems (m) | ['nød,brɛms] |

compartment	kupé (m)	[kʉ'pe]
berth	køye (m/f)	['køjə]
upper berth	overkøye (m/f)	['ɔvər,køjə]
lower berth	underkøye (m/f)	['ʉnər,køjə]
bed linen, bedding	sengetøy (n)	['sɛŋə,tøj]

ticket	billett (m)	[bi'let]
schedule	rutetabell (m)	['rʉtə,tɑ'bɛl]
information display	informasjonstavle (m/f)	[infɔrmɑ'ṣʊns ,tɑvlə]

to leave, to depart	å avgå	[ɔ 'avgɔ]
departure (of train)	avgang (m)	['av,gɑŋ]
to arrive (ab. train)	å ankomme	[ɔ 'an,kɔmə]
arrival	ankomst (m)	['an,kɔmst]
to arrive by train	å ankomme med toget	[ɔ 'an,kɔmə me 'tɔge]
to get on the train	å gå på toget	[ɔ 'gɔ pɔ 'tɔge]

to get off the train	å gå av toget	[ɔ 'gɔ ɑ: 'tɔgə]
train wreck	togulykke (m/n)	['tɔg ʉ'lʏkə]
to derail (vi)	å spore av	[ɔ 'spʉrə ɑ:]
steam locomotive	damplokomotiv (n)	['damp lʊkɔmɔ'tiv]
stoker, fireman	fyrbøter (m)	['fyr‚bøtər]
firebox	fyrrom (n)	['fyr‚rʉm]
coal	kull (n)	['kʉl]

26. Ship

| ship | skip (n) | ['şip] |
| vessel | fartøy (n) | ['fɑ:‚tøj] |

steamship	dampskip (n)	['damp‚şip]
riverboat	elvebåt (m)	['ɛlvə‚bɔt]
cruise ship	cruiseskip (n)	['krʉs‚şip]
cruiser	krysser (m)	['krʏsər]

yacht	jakt (m/f)	['jakt]
tugboat	bukserbåt (m)	[bʉk'ser‚bɔt]
barge	lastepram (m)	['lastə‚pram]
ferry	ferje, ferge (m/f)	['færjə], ['færgə]

| sailing ship | seilbåt (n) | ['sæjl‚bɔt] |
| brigantine | brigantin (m) | [brigan'tin] |

| ice breaker | isbryter (m) | ['is‚brytər] |
| submarine | ubåt (m) | ['ʉ:‚bɔt] |

boat (flat-bottomed ~)	båt (m)	['bɔt]
dinghy	jolle (m/f)	['jɔlə]
lifeboat	livbåt (m)	['liv‚bɔt]
motorboat	motorbåt (m)	['mɔtʉr‚bɔt]

captain	kaptein (m)	[kap'tæjn]
seaman	matros (m)	[ma'trʊs]
sailor	sjømann (m)	['şø‚man]
crew	besetning (m/f)	[be'sɛtniŋ]

boatswain	båtsmann (m)	['bɔs‚man]
ship's boy	skipsgutt, jungmann (m)	['şips‚gʉt], ['jʉŋ‚man]
cook	kokk (m)	['kʊk]
ship's doctor	skipslege (m)	['şips‚legə]

deck	dekk (n)	['dɛk]
mast	mast (m/f)	['mast]
sail	seil (n)	['sæjl]

| hold | lasterom (n) | ['lastə‚rʉm] |
| bow (prow) | baug (m) | ['bæu] |

stern	akterende (m)	['aktəˌrɛnə]
oar	åre (m)	['oːrə]
screw propeller	propell (m)	[prʊ'pɛl]

cabin	hytte (m)	['hʏtə]
wardroom	offisersmesse (m/f)	[ɔfi'sɛrsˌmɛsə]
engine room	maskinrom (n)	[ma'ʂinˌrʊm]
bridge	kommandobro (m/f)	[kɔ'mandʊˌbrʊ]
radio room	radiorom (m)	['radiʊˌrʊm]
wave (radio)	bølge (m)	['bølgə]
logbook	loggbok (m/f)	['lɔɡˌbʊk]

spyglass	langkikkert (m)	['laŋˌkikeːt]
bell	klokke (m/f)	['klɔkə]
flag	flagg (n)	['flaɡ]

| hawser (mooring ~) | trosse (m/f) | ['trʊsə] |
| knot (bowline, etc.) | knute (m) | ['knʉtə] |

| deckrails | rekkverk (n) | ['rɛkˌværk] |
| gangway | landgang (m) | ['lanˌɡaŋ] |

anchor	anker (n)	['ankər]
to weigh anchor	å lette anker	[ɔ 'letə 'ankər]
to drop anchor	å kaste anker	[ɔ 'kastə 'ankər]
anchor chain	ankerkjetting (m)	['ankərˌçɛtiŋ]

port (harbor)	havn (m/f)	['havn]
quay, wharf	kai (m/f)	['kaj]
to berth (moor)	å fortøye	[ɔ fɔ:'tøjə]
to cast off	å kaste loss	[ɔ 'kastə lɔs]

trip, voyage	reise (m/f)	['ræjsə]
cruise (sea trip)	cruise (n)	['krʉs]
course (route)	kurs (m)	['kʉʂ]
route (itinerary)	rute (m/f)	['rʉtə]

fairway (safe water channel)	seilrende (m)	['sæjlˌrɛnə]
shallows	grunne (m/f)	['ɡrʉnə]
to run aground	å gå på grunn	[ɔ 'ɡɔ pɔ 'ɡrʉn]

storm	storm (m)	['stɔrm]
signal	signal (n)	[siŋ'nal]
to sink (vi)	å synke	[ɔ 'sʏnkə]
Man overboard!	Mann over bord!	['man ˌɔvər 'bʊr]
SOS (distress signal)	SOS (n)	[ɛsʊ'ɛs]
ring buoy	livbøye (m/f)	['livˌbøjə]

CITY

27. Urban transportation

bus	buss (m)	['bʉs]
streetcar	trikk (m)	['trik]
trolley bus	trolleybuss (m)	['trɔli,bʉs]
route (of bus, etc.)	rute (m/f)	['rʉtə]
number (e.g., bus ~)	nummer (n)	['nʉmər]

to go by ...	å kjøre med ...	[ɔ 'çœːrə me ...]
to get on (~ the bus)	å gå på ...	[ɔ 'gɔ pɔ ...]
to get off ...	å gå av ...	[ɔ 'gɔ ɑː ...]

stop (e.g., bus ~)	holdeplass (m)	['hɔlə,plɑs]
next stop	neste holdeplass (m)	['nɛstə 'hɔlə,plɑs]
terminus	endestasjon (m)	['ɛnə,stɑ'ʂʉn]
schedule	rutetabell (m)	['rʉtə,tɑ'bɛl]
to wait (vt)	å vente	[ɔ 'vɛntə]

ticket	billett (m)	[bi'let]
fare	billettpris (m)	[bi'let,pris]

cashier (ticket seller)	kasserer (m)	[kɑ'serər]
ticket inspection	billettkontroll (m)	[bi'let kʉn,trɔl]
ticket inspector	billett inspektør (m)	[bi'let inspɛk'tør]

to be late (for ...)	å komme for sent	[ɔ 'kɔmə fɔ'sɛnt]
to miss (~ the train, etc.)	å komme for sent til ...	[ɔ 'kɔmə fɔ'sɛnt til ...]
to be in a hurry	å skynde seg	[ɔ 'ʂynə sæj]

taxi, cab	drosje (m/f), taxi (m)	['drɔʂɛ], ['tɑksi]
taxi driver	taxisjåfør (m)	['tɑksi ʂɔ'før]
by taxi	med taxi	[me 'tɑksi]
taxi stand	taxiholdeplass (m)	['tɑksi 'hɔlə,plɑs]
to call a taxi	å taxi bestellen	[ɔ 'tɑksi be'stɛlən]
to take a taxi	å ta taxi	[ɔ 'tɑ ,tɑksi]

traffic	trafikk (m)	[trɑ'fik]
traffic jam	trafikkork (m)	[trɑ'fik,kɔrk]
rush hour	rushtid (m/f)	['rʉʂ,tid]
to park (vi)	å parkere	[ɔ pɑr'kerə]
to park (vt)	å parkere	[ɔ pɑr'kerə]
parking lot	parkeringsplass (m)	[pɑr'keriŋs,plɑs]
subway	tunnelbane, T-bane (m)	['tʉnəl,banə], ['tɛː,banə]
station	stasjon (m)	[stɑ'ʂʉn]

to take the subway	å kjøre med T-bane	[ɔ 'çœːrə me 'tɛːˌbɑnə]
train	tog (n)	['tɔg]
train station	togstasjon (m)	['tɔgˌstɑ'ʂʊn]

28. City. Life in the city

city, town	by (m)	['by]
capital city	hovedstad (m)	['hʊvədˌstɑd]
village	landsby (m)	['lɑnsˌby]

city map	bykart (n)	['byˌkɑːt]
downtown	sentrum (n)	['sɛntrum]
suburb	forstad (m)	['fɔˌʂtɑd]
suburban (adj)	forstads-	['fɔˌʂtɑds-]

outskirts	utkant (m)	['ʉtˌkɑnt]
environs (suburbs)	omegner (m pl)	['ɔmˌæjnər]
city block	kvarter (n)	[kvɑːˈʈer]
residential block (area)	boligkvarter (n)	['bʊliˌkvɑːˈʈer]

traffic	trafikk (m)	[trɑˈfik]
traffic lights	trafikklys (n)	[trɑˈfikˌlys]
public transportation	offentlig transport (m)	['ɔfentli trɑnsˈpɔːt]
intersection	veikryss (n)	['væjkrʏs]

crosswalk	fotgjengerovergang (m)	['fʊtˌjɛŋer 'ɔvərˌgɑŋ]
pedestrian underpass	undergang (m)	['ʉnərˌgɑŋ]
to cross (~ the street)	å gå over	[ɔ 'gɔ 'ɔvər]
pedestrian	fotgjenger (m)	['fʊtˌjɛŋər]
sidewalk	fortau (n)	['fɔːˌtɑʊ]

bridge	bro (m/f)	['brʊ]
embankment (river walk)	kai (m/f)	['kɑj]
fountain	fontene (m)	['fʊntnə]

allée (garden walkway)	allé (m)	[ɑˈleː]
park	park (m)	['pɑrk]
boulevard	bulevard (m)	[buleˈvɑr]
square	torg (n)	['tɔr]
avenue (wide street)	aveny (m)	[aveˈny]
street	gate (m/f)	['gɑtə]
side street	sidegate (m/f)	['sidəˌgɑtə]
dead end	blindgate (m/f)	['blinˌgɑtə]

house	hus (n)	['hʉs]
building	bygning (m/f)	['bʏgniŋ]
skyscraper	skyskraper (m)	['ʂyˌskrɑpər]

| facade | fasade (m) | [faˈsɑdə] |
| roof | tak (n) | ['tɑk] |

window	vindu (n)	['vindʉ]
arch	bue (m)	['bʉːə]
column	søyle (m)	['søjlə]
corner	hjørne (n)	['jœːŋə]

store window	utstillingsvindu (n)	['ʉt‚stiliŋs 'vindʉ]
signboard (store sign, etc.)	skilt (n)	['ʂilt]
poster	plakat (m)	[plɑ'kɑt]
advertising poster	reklameplakat (m)	[rɛ'klɑmə‚plɑ'kɑt]
billboard	reklametavle (m/f)	[rɛ'klɑmə‚tɑvlə]

garbage, trash	søppel (m/f/n), avfall (n)	['sœpəl], ['ɑv‚fɑl]
trashcan (public ~)	søppelkasse (m/f)	['sœpəl‚kɑsə]
to litter (vi)	å kaste søppel	[ɔ 'kɑstə 'sœpəl]
garbage dump	søppelfylling (m/f), deponi (n)	['sœpəl‚fʏliŋ], [‚depɔ'ni]

phone booth	telefonboks (m)	[tele'fun‚bɔks]
lamppost	lyktestolpe (m)	['lʏktə‚stɔlpə]
bench (park ~)	benk (m)	['bɛŋk]

police officer	politi (m)	[pʊli'ti]
police	politi (n)	[pʊli'ti]
beggar	tigger (m)	['tigər]
homeless (n)	hjemløs	['jɛm‚løs]

29. Urban institutions

store	forretning, butikk (m)	[fɔ'rɛtniŋ], [bʉ'tik]
drugstore, pharmacy	apotek (n)	[apʊ'tek]
eyeglass store	optikk (m)	[ɔp'tik]
shopping mall	kjøpesenter (n)	['çœpə‚sɛntər]
supermarket	supermarked (n)	['sʉpə‚market]

bakery	bakeri (n)	[bake'ri]
baker	baker (m)	['bakər]
pastry shop	konditori (n)	[kʊnditɔ'ri]
grocery store	matbutikk (m)	['mɑtbʉ‚tik]
butcher shop	slakterbutikk (m)	['ʂlɑktəbʉ‚tik]

| produce store | grønnsaksbutikk (m) | ['grœn‚saks bʉ'tik] |
| market | marked (n) | ['markəd] |

coffee house	kafé, kaffebar (m)	[ka'fe], ['kafə‚bar]
restaurant	restaurant (m)	[rɛstʊ'rɑŋ]
pub, bar	pub (m)	['pʉb]
pizzeria	pizzeria (m)	[pitsə'ria]

| hair salon | frisørsalong (m) | [fri'sør sa‚lɔŋ] |
| post office | post (m) | ['pɔst] |

dry cleaners	renseri (n)	[rɛnse'ri]
photo studio	fotostudio (n)	['fotoˌstʉdiɔ]
shoe store	skobutikk (m)	['skʉˌbʉ'tik]
bookstore	bokhandel (m)	['bʉkˌhandəl]
sporting goods store	idrettsbutikk (m)	['idrɛts bʉ'tik]
clothes repair shop	reparasjon (m) av klær	[repara'ʂʉn aː ˌklær]
formal wear rental	leie (m/f) av klær	['læjə aː ˌklær]
video rental store	filmutleie (m/f)	['filmˌʉt'læje]
circus	sirkus (m/n)	['sirkʉs]
zoo	zoo, dyrepark (m)	['sʉː], [dyrə'park]
movie theater	kino (m)	['çinʉ]
museum	museum (n)	[mʉ'seum]
library	bibliotek (n)	[bibliʉ'tek]
theater	teater (n)	[te'atər]
opera (opera house)	opera (m)	['ʉpera]
nightclub	nattklubb (m)	['natˌklʉb]
casino	kasino (n)	[ka'sinʉ]
mosque	moské (m)	[mʉ'ske]
synagogue	synagoge (m)	[syna'gʉgə]
cathedral	katedral (m)	[kate'dral]
temple	tempel (n)	['tɛmpəl]
church	kirke (m/f)	['çirkə]
college	institutt (n)	[insti'tʉt]
university	universitet (n)	[ʉnivæʂi'tet]
school	skole (m/f)	['skʉlə]
prefecture	prefektur (n)	[prɛfɛk'tʉr]
city hall	rådhus (n)	['rɔdˌhʉs]
hotel	hotell (n)	[hʉ'tɛl]
bank	bank (m)	['bank]
embassy	ambassade (m)	[amba'sadə]
travel agency	reisebyrå (n)	['ræjsə byˌro]
information office	opplysningskontor (n)	[ɔp'lʏsniŋs kʉn'tʉr]
currency exchange	vekslingskontor (n)	['vɛkʂliŋs kʉn'tʉr]
subway	tunnelbane, T-bane (m)	['tʉnəlˌbanə], ['tɛːˌbanə]
hospital	sykehus (n)	['sykəˌhʉs]
gas station	bensinstasjon (m)	[bɛn'sinˌsta'ʂʉn]
parking lot	parkeringsplass (m)	[par'keriŋsˌplas]

30. Signs

signboard (store sign, etc.)	skilt (n)	['ʂilt]
notice (door sign, etc.)	innskrift (m/f)	['inˌskrift]

poster	**plakat, poster** (m)	['plɑˌkat], ['pɔstər]
direction sign	**veiviser** (m)	['væjˌvisər]
arrow (sign)	**pil** (m/f)	['pil]

caution	**advarsel** (m)	['adˌvaʂəl]
warning sign	**varselskilt** (n)	['vaʂəlˌʂilt]
to warn (vt)	**å varsle**	[ɔ 'vaʂlə]

rest day (weekly ~)	**fridag** (m)	['friˌdɑ]
timetable (schedule)	**rutetabell** (m)	['rʉtəˌtɑ'bɛl]
opening hours	**åpningstider** (m/f pl)	['ɔpniŋsˌtidər]

WELCOME!	**VELKOMMEN!**	['vɛlˌkɔmən]
ENTRANCE	**INNGANG**	['inˌgɑŋ]
EXIT	**UTGANG**	['ʉtˌgɑŋ]

PUSH	**SKYV**	['ʂyv]
PULL	**TREKK**	['trɛk]
OPEN	**ÅPENT**	['ɔpənt]
CLOSED	**STENGT**	['stɛŋt]

| WOMEN | **DAMER** | ['damər] |
| MEN | **HERRER** | ['hærər] |

DISCOUNTS	**RABATT**	[ra'bat]
SALE	**SALG**	['salg]
NEW!	**NYTT!**	['nʏt]
FREE	**GRATIS**	['gratis]

ATTENTION!	**FORSIKTIG!**	[fʊ'ʂiktə]
NO VACANCIES	**INGEN LEDIGE ROM**	['iŋən 'lediə rʊm]
RESERVED	**RESERVERT**	[resɛr'vɛ:t]

| ADMINISTRATION | **ADMINISTRASJON** | [administra'ʂʊn] |
| STAFF ONLY | **KUN FOR ANSATTE** | ['kʉn fɔr an'satə] |

BEWARE OF THE DOG!	**VOKT DEM FOR HUNDEN**	['vɔkt dem fɔ 'hʉnən]
NO SMOKING	**RØYKING FORBUDT**	['røjkiŋ fɔr'bʉt]
DO NOT TOUCH!	**IKKE RØR!**	['ikə 'rør]

DANGEROUS	**FARLIG**	['fɑ:l[i]
DANGER	**FARE**	['farə]
HIGH VOLTAGE	**HØYSPENNING**	['højˌspɛniŋ]

| NO SWIMMING! | **BADING FORBUDT** | ['badiŋ fɔr'bʉt] |
| OUT OF ORDER | **I USTAND** | [i 'ʉˌstan] |

FLAMMABLE	**BRANNFARLIG**	['branˌfɑ:l[i]
FORBIDDEN	**FORBUDT**	[fɔr'bʉt]
NO TRESPASSING!	**INGEN INNKJØRING**	['iŋən 'inˌçœriŋ]
WET PAINT	**NYMALT**	['nyˌmalt]

31. Shopping

to buy (purchase)	**å kjøpe**	[ɔ 'çœ:pə]
purchase	**innkjøp** (n)	['in‚çœp]
to go shopping	**å gå shopping**	[ɔ 'gɔ ‚sɔpiŋ]
shopping	**shopping** (m)	['şɔpiŋ]
to be open (ab. store)	**å være åpen**	[ɔ 'værə 'ɔpən]
to be closed	**å være stengt**	[ɔ 'værə 'stɛŋt]
footwear, shoes	**skotøy** (n)	['skʊtøj]
clothes, clothing	**klær** (n)	['klær]
cosmetics	**kosmetikk** (m)	[kʊsme'tik]
food products	**matvarer** (m/f pl)	['mɑt‚vɑrər]
gift, present	**gave** (m/f)	['gɑvə]
salesman	**forselger** (m)	[fɔ'şɛlər]
saleswoman	**forselger** (m)	[fɔ'şɛlər]
check out, cash desk	**kasse** (m/f)	['kɑsə]
mirror	**speil** (n)	['spæjl]
counter (store ~)	**disk** (m)	['disk]
fitting room	**prøverom** (n)	['prøvə‚rʊm]
to try on	**å prøve**	[ɔ 'prøvə]
to fit (ab. dress, etc.)	**å passe**	[ɔ 'pɑsə]
to like (I like ...)	**å like**	[ɔ 'likə]
price	**pris** (m)	['pris]
price tag	**prislapp** (m)	['pris‚lɑp]
to cost (vt)	**å koste**	[ɔ 'kɔstə]
How much?	**Hvor mye?**	[vʊr 'mye]
discount	**rabatt** (m)	[rɑ'bɑt]
inexpensive (adj)	**billig**	['bili]
cheap (adj)	**billig**	['bili]
expensive (adj)	**dyr**	['dyr]
It's expensive	**Det er dyrt**	[de ær 'dy:t]
rental (n)	**utleie** (m/f)	['ʉt‚læje]
to rent (~ a tuxedo)	**å leie**	[ɔ 'læje]
credit (trade credit)	**kreditt** (m)	[krɛ'dit]
on credit (adv)	**på kreditt**	[pɔ krɛ'dit]

CLOTHING & ACCESSORIES

32. Outerwear. Coats

clothes	**klær** (n)	['klær]
outerwear	**yttertøy** (n)	['ytə͵tøj]
winter clothing	**vinterklær** (n pl)	['vintər͵klær]
coat (overcoat)	**frakk** (m), **kåpe** (m/f)	['frak], ['ko:pə]
fur coat	**pels** (m), **pelskåpe** (m/f)	['pɛls], ['pɛls͵ko:pə]
fur jacket	**pelsjakke** (m/f)	['pɛls͵jakə]
down coat	**dunjakke** (m/f)	['dun͵jakə]
jacket (e.g., leather ~)	**jakke** (m/f)	['jakə]
raincoat (trenchcoat, etc.)	**regnfrakk** (m)	['ræjn͵frak]
waterproof (adj)	**vanntett**	['van͵tɛt]

33. Men's & women's clothing

shirt (button shirt)	**skjorte** (m/f)	['sɕœ:ʈə]
pants	**bukse** (m)	['buksə]
jeans	**jeans** (m)	['dʒins]
suit jacket	**dressjakke** (m/f)	['drɛs͵jakə]
suit	**dress** (m)	['drɛs]
dress (frock)	**kjole** (m)	['çulə]
skirt	**skjørt** (n)	['sø:ʈ]
blouse	**bluse** (m)	['blusə]
knitted jacket (cardigan, etc.)	**strikket trøye** (m/f)	['strikə 'trøjə]
jacket (of woman's suit)	**blazer** (m)	['blæsər]
T-shirt	**T-skjorte** (m/f)	['te͵sɕœ:ʈə]
shorts (short trousers)	**shorts** (m)	['ʂɔ:ʈs]
tracksuit	**treningsdrakt** (m/f)	['treniŋs͵drakt]
bathrobe	**badekåpe** (m/f)	['badə͵ko:pə]
pajamas	**pyjamas** (m)	[py'ʂamas]
sweater	**sweater** (m)	['svɛtər]
pullover	**pullover** (m)	[pu'lɔvər]
vest	**vest** (m)	['vɛst]
tailcoat	**livkjole** (m)	['liv͵çulə]
tuxedo	**smoking** (m)	['smɔkiŋ]

uniform	uniform (m)	[ʉni'fɔrm]
workwear	arbeidsklær (n pl)	['ɑrbæjds̩klær]
overalls	kjeledress, overall (m)	['çelə̩drɛs], ['ɔvɛr̩ɔl]
coat (e.g., doctor's smock)	kittel (m)	['çitəl]

34. Clothing. Underwear

underwear	undertøy (n)	['ʉnə̩tøj]
boxers, briefs	underbukse (m/f)	['ʉnər̩bʉksə]
panties	truse (m/f)	['trʉsə]
undershirt (A-shirt)	undertrøye (m/f)	['ʉnə̩trøjə]
socks	sokker (m pl)	['sɔkər]

nightgown	nattkjole (m)	['nat̩çulə]
bra	behå (m)	['be̩hɔ]
knee highs	knestrømper (m/f pl)	['knɛ̩strømpər]
(knee-high socks)		
pantyhose	strømpebukse (m/f)	['strømpə̩bʉksə]
stockings (thigh highs)	strømper (m/f pl)	['strømpər]
bathing suit	badedrakt (m/f)	['bɑdə̩drɑkt]

35. Headwear

hat	hatt (m)	['hat]
fedora	hatt (m)	['hat]
baseball cap	baseball cap (m)	['bɛjsbɔl kɛp]
flatcap	sikspens (m)	['sikspens]

beret	alpelue, baskerlue (m/f)	['ɑlpə̩lʉə], ['bɑskə̩lʉə]
hood	hette (m/f)	['hɛtə]
panama hat	panamahatt (m)	['pɑnɑmɑ̩hat]
knit cap (knitted hat)	strikket lue (m/f)	['strikə̩lʉə]

headscarf	skaut (n)	['skaʉt]
women's hat	hatt (m)	['hat]
hard hat	hjelm (m)	['jɛlm]
garrison cap	båtlue (m/f)	['bɔt̩lʉə]
helmet	hjelm (m)	['jɛlm]

| derby | bowlerhatt, skalk (m) | ['bɔuler̩hat], ['skɑlk] |
| top hat | flosshatt (m) | ['flɔs̩hat] |

36. Footwear

| footwear | skotøy (n) | ['skʉtøj] |
| shoes (men's shoes) | skor (m pl) | ['skʉr] |

shoes (women's shoes)	pumps (m pl)	['pumps]
boots (e.g., cowboy ~)	støvler (m pl)	['støvlər]
slippers	tøfler (m pl)	['tøflər]

tennis shoes (e.g., Nike ~)	tennissko (m pl)	['tɛnis‚skʊ]
sneakers	canvas sko (m pl)	['kɑnvɑs ‚skʊ]
(e.g., Converse ~)		
sandals	sandaler (m pl)	[sɑn'dɑlər]

cobbler (shoe repairer)	skomaker (m)	['skʊ‚mɑkər]
heel	hæl (m)	['hæl]
pair (of shoes)	par (n)	['pɑr]

shoestring	skolisse (m/f)	['skʊ‚lisə]
to lace (vt)	å snøre	[ɔ 'snørə]
shoehorn	skohorn (n)	['skʊ‚huːŋ]
shoe polish	skokrem (m)	['skʊ‚krɛm]

37. Personal accessories

gloves	hansker (m pl)	['hɑnskər]
mittens	votter (m pl)	['vɔtər]
scarf (muffler)	skjerf (n)	['ʂærf]

glasses (eyeglasses)	briller (m pl)	['brilər]
frame (eyeglass ~)	innfatning (m/f)	['in‚fɑtniŋ]
umbrella	paraply (m)	[pɑrɑ'ply]
walking stick	stokk (m)	['stɔk]

| hairbrush | hårbørste (m) | ['hɔr‚bœʂtə] |
| fan | vifte (m/f) | ['viftə] |

| tie (necktie) | slips (n) | ['slips] |
| bow tie | sløyfe (m/f) | ['ʂløjfə] |

| suspenders | bukseseler (m pl) | ['bʉkse'selər] |
| handkerchief | lommetørkle (n) | ['lʉmə‚tœrklə] |

| comb | kam (m) | ['kɑm] |
| barrette | hårspenne (m/f/n) | ['hoːr‚spɛnə] |

| hairpin | hårnål (m/f) | ['hoːr‚nol] |
| buckle | spenne (m/f/n) | ['spɛnə] |

| belt | belte (m) | ['bɛltə] |
| shoulder strap | skulderreim, rem (m/f) | ['skʉldə‚ræjm], ['rem] |

bag (handbag)	veske (m/f)	['vɛskə]
purse	håndveske (m/f)	['hɔn‚vɛskə]
backpack	ryggsekk (m)	['rʏg‚sɛk]

38. Clothing. Miscellaneous

fashion	mote (m)	['mʊtə]
in vogue (adj)	moteriktig	['mʊtə‚rikti]
fashion designer	moteskaper (m)	['mʊtə‚skɑpər]

collar	krage (m)	['krɑgə]
pocket	lomme (m/f)	['lʊmə]
pocket (as adj)	lomme-	['lʊmə-]
sleeve	erme (n)	['ærmə]
hanging loop	hempe (m)	['hɛmpə]
fly (on trousers)	gylf, buksesmekk (m)	['gylf], ['bʊksə‚smɛk]

zipper (fastener)	glidelås (m/n)	['glidə‚lɔs]
fastener	hekte (m/f), knepping (m)	['hɛktə], ['knɛpiŋ]
button	knapp (m)	['knɑp]
buttonhole	klapphull (n)	['klɑp‚hʊl]
to come off (ab. button)	å falle av	[ɔ 'fɑlə ɑ:]

to sew (vi, vt)	å sy	[ɔ 'sy]
to embroider (vi, vt)	å brodere	[ɔ brʊ'derə]
embroidery	broderi (n)	[brʊde'ri]
sewing needle	synål (m/f)	['sy‚nɔl]
thread	tråd (m)	['trɔ]
seam	søm (m)	['søm]

to get dirty (vi)	å skitne seg til	[ɔ 'ʂitnə sæj til]
stain (mark, spot)	flekk (m)	['flek]
to crease, crumple (vi)	å bli skrukkete	[ɔ 'bli 'skrʊketə]
to tear, to rip (vt)	å rive	[ɔ 'rivə]
clothes moth	møll (m/n)	['møl]

39. Personal care. Cosmetics

toothpaste	tannpasta (m)	['tɑn‚pɑstɑ]
toothbrush	tannbørste (m)	['tɑn‚bœʂtə]
to brush one's teeth	å pusse tennene	[ɔ 'pʉsə 'tɛnənə]

razor	høvel (m)	['høvəl]
shaving cream	barberkrem (m)	[bɑr'bɛr‚krɛm]
to shave (vi)	å barbere seg	[ɔ bɑr'berə sæj]

soap	såpe (m/f)	['so:pə]
shampoo	sjampo (m)	['ʂɑm‚pʊ]

scissors	saks (m/f)	['sɑks]
nail file	neglefil (m/f)	['nɛjlə‚fil]
nail clippers	negleklipper (m)	['nɛjlə‚klipər]
tweezers	pinsett (m)	[pin'sɛt]

cosmetics	kosmetikk (m)	[kʊsmeˈtik]
face mask	ansiktsmaske (m/f)	[ˈansiktsˌmaskə]
manicure	manikyr (m)	[maniˈkyr]
to have a manicure	å få manikyr	[ɔ ˈfɔ maniˈkyr]
pedicure	pedikyr (m)	[pediˈkyr]

make-up bag	sminkeveske (m/f)	[ˈsminkəˌvɛskə]
face powder	pudder (n)	[ˈpʉdər]
powder compact	pudderdåse (m)	[ˈpʉdərˌdoːsə]
blusher	rouge (m)	[ˈruːʂ]

perfume (bottled)	parfyme (m)	[parˈfymə]
toilet water (lotion)	eau de toilette (m)	[ˈɔ də twaˈlet]
lotion	lotion (m)	[ˈlɔʉʂɛn]
cologne	eau de cologne (m)	[ˈɔ də kɔˈlɔɲ]

eyeshadow	øyeskygge (m)	[ˈøjəˌʂygə]
eyeliner	eyeliner (m)	[ˈaːjˌlajnər]
mascara	maskara (m)	[maˈskara]

lipstick	leppestift (m)	[ˈlepəˌstift]
nail polish, enamel	neglelakk (m)	[ˈnɛjləˌlak]
hair spray	hårlakk (m)	[ˈhoːrˌlak]
deodorant	deodorant (m)	[deudʉˈrant]

cream	krem (m)	[ˈkrɛm]
face cream	ansiktskrem (m)	[ˈansiktsˌkrɛm]
hand cream	håndkrem (m)	[ˈhɔnˌkrɛm]
anti-wrinkle cream	antirynkekrem (m)	[antiˈrʏnkəˌkrɛm]
day cream	dagkrem (m)	[ˈdagˌkrɛm]
night cream	nattkrem (m)	[ˈnatˌkrɛm]
day (as adj)	dag-	[ˈdag-]
night (as adj)	natt-	[ˈnat-]

tampon	tampong (m)	[tamˈpɔŋ]
toilet paper (toilet roll)	toalettpapir (n)	[tʊaˈlet paˈpir]
hair dryer	hårføner (m)	[ˈhoːrˌfønər]

40. Watches. Clocks

watch (wristwatch)	armbåndsur (n)	[ˈarmbɔnsˌʉr]
dial	urskive (m/f)	[ˈʉːˌʂivə]
hand (of clock, watch)	viser (m)	[ˈvisər]
metal watch band	armbånd (n)	[ˈarmˌbɔn]
watch strap	rem (m/f)	[ˈrem]

battery	batteri (n)	[batɛˈri]
to be dead (battery)	å bli utladet	[ɔ ˈbli ˈʉtˌladət]
to change a battery	å skifte batteriene	[ɔ ˈʂiftə batɛˈriene]
to run fast	å gå for fort	[ɔ ˈgɔ fɔ ˈfoːʈ]

to run slow	**å gå for sakte**	[ɔ 'gɔ fɔ 'sɑktə]
wall clock	**veggur** (n)	['vɛg‚ʉr]
hourglass	**timeglass** (n)	['timə‚glɑs]
sundial	**solur** (n)	['sʊl‚ʉr]
alarm clock	**vekkerklokka** (m/f)	['vɛkər‚klɔkɑ]
watchmaker	**urmaker** (m)	['ʉr‚mɑkər]
to repair (vt)	**å reparere**	[ɔ repɑ'rerə]

EVERYDAY EXPERIENCE

41. Money

money	penger (m pl)	['pɛŋər]
currency exchange	veksling (m/f)	['vɛkşliŋ]
exchange rate	kurs (m)	['kuş]
ATM	minibank (m)	['mini,bank]
coin	mynt (m)	['mʏnt]
dollar	dollar (m)	['dɔlar]
euro	euro (m)	['ɛurʊ]
lira	lira (m)	['lire]
Deutschmark	mark (m/f)	['mark]
franc	franc (m)	['fran]
pound sterling	pund sterling (m)	['pʉn stɛ:'ɭiŋ]
yen	yen (m)	['jɛn]
debt	skyld (m/f), gjeld (m)	['şyl], ['jɛl]
debtor	skyldner (m)	['şylnər]
to lend (money)	å låne ut	[ɔ 'lo:nə ʉt]
to borrow (vi, vt)	å låne	[ɔ 'lo:nə]
bank	bank (m)	['bank]
account	konto (m)	['kɔntʊ]
to deposit (vt)	å sette inn	[ɔ 'sɛtə in]
to deposit into the account	å sette inn på kontoen	[ɔ 'sɛtə in pɔ 'kɔntʊən]
to withdraw (vt)	å ta ut fra kontoen	[ɔ 'ta ʉt fra 'kɔntʊən]
credit card	kredittkort (n)	[krɛ'dit,kɔ:t]
cash	kontanter (m pl)	[kʊn'tantər]
check	sjekk (m)	['şɛk]
to write a check	å skrive en sjekk	[ɔ 'skrivə en 'şɛk]
checkbook	sjekkbok (m/f)	['şɛk,bʊk]
wallet	lommebok (m)	['lʊmə,bʊk]
change purse	pung (m)	['pʉŋ]
safe	safe, seif (m)	['sɛjf]
heir	arving (m)	['arviŋ]
inheritance	arv (m)	['arv]
fortune (wealth)	formue (m)	['fɔr,mʉə]
lease	leie (m)	['læje]
rent (money)	husleie (m/f)	['hʉs,læje]

to rent (sth from sb)	å leie	[ɔ 'læjə]
price	pris (m)	['pris]
cost	kostnad (m)	['kɔstnɑd]
sum	sum (m)	['sʉm]

to spend (vt)	å bruke	[ɔ 'brʉkə]
expenses	utgifter (m/f pl)	['ʉtˌjiftər]
to economize (vi, vt)	å spare	[ɔ 'spɑrə]
economical	sparsom	['spɑʂɔm]

to pay (vi, vt)	å betale	[ɔ be'tɑlə]
payment	betaling (m/f)	[be'tɑliŋ]
change (give the ~)	vekslepenger (pl)	['vɛkʂləˌpɛŋər]

tax	skatt (m)	['skɑt]
fine	bot (m/f)	['bʊt]
to fine (vt)	å bøtelegge	[ɔ 'bøtəˌlegə]

42. Post. Postal service

post office	post (m)	['pɔst]
mail (letters, etc.)	post (m)	['pɔst]
mailman	postbud (n)	['pɔstˌbʉd]
opening hours	åpningstider (m/f pl)	['ɔpniŋsˌtidər]

letter	brev (n)	['brev]
registered letter	rekommandert brev (n)	[rekʉmɑn'dɛːt ˌbrev]
postcard	postkort (n)	['pɔstˌkɔːt]
telegram	telegram (n)	[tele'grɑm]
package (parcel)	postpakke (m/f)	['pɔstˌpɑkə]
money transfer	pengeoverføring (m/f)	['pɛŋə 'ɔvərˌføriŋ]

to receive (vt)	å motta	[ɔ 'mɔtɑ]
to send (vt)	å sende	[ɔ 'sɛnə]
sending	avsending (m)	['ɑfˌsɛniŋ]

address	adresse (m)	[ɑ'drɛsə]
ZIP code	postnummer (n)	['pɔstˌnʉmər]
sender	avsender (m)	['ɑfˌsɛnər]
receiver	mottaker (m)	['mɔtˌtɑkər]

name (first name)	fornavn (n)	['fɔrˌnɑvn]
surname (last name)	etternavn (n)	['ɛtəˌnɑvn]

postage rate	tariff (m)	[tɑ'rif]
standard (adj)	vanlig	['vɑnli]
economical (adj)	økonomisk	[økʉ'nɔmisk]

weight	vekt (m)	['vɛkt]
to weigh (~ letters)	å veie	[ɔ 'væjə]

envelope	konvolutt (m)	[kʊnvʊ'lʉt]
postage stamp	frimerke (n)	['fri,mærkə]
to stamp an envelope	å sette på frimerke	[ɔ 'sɛtə pɔ 'fri,mærkə]

43. Banking

| bank | bank (m) | ['bɑnk] |
| branch (of bank, etc.) | avdeling (m) | ['ɑv,deliŋ] |

| bank clerk, consultant | konsulent (m) | [kʊnsʉ'lent] |
| manager (director) | forstander (m) | [fɔ'ʂtandər] |

bank account	bankkonto (m)	['bɑnk,kɔntʊ]
account number	kontonummer (n)	['kɔntʊ,nʉmər]
checking account	sjekkonto (m)	['ʂɛk,kɔntʊ]
savings account	sparekonto (m)	['spɑrə,kɔntʊ]

| to open an account | å åpne en konto | [ɔ 'ɔpnə en 'kɔntʊ] |
| to close the account | å lukke kontoen | [ɔ 'lʉkə 'kɔntʊən] |

| to deposit into the account | å sette inn på kontoen | [ɔ 'sɛtə in pɔ 'kɔntʊən] |
| to withdraw (vt) | å ta ut fra kontoen | [ɔ 'tɑ ʉt frɑ 'kɔntʊən] |

| deposit | innskudd (n) | ['in,skʉd] |
| to make a deposit | å sette inn | [ɔ 'sɛtə in] |

| wire transfer | overføring (m/f) | ['ɔvər,føriŋ] |
| to wire, to transfer | å overføre | [ɔ 'ɔvər,førə] |

| sum | sum (m) | ['sʉm] |
| How much? | Hvor mye? | [vʊr 'mye] |

| signature | underskrift (m/f) | ['ʉnə,skrift] |
| to sign (vt) | å underskrive | [ɔ 'ʉnə,skrivə] |

| credit card | kredittkort (n) | [krɛ'dit,kɔːʈ] |
| code (PIN code) | kode (m) | ['kʊdə] |

| credit card number | kreditkortnummer (n) | [krɛ'dit,kɔːʈ 'nʉmər] |
| ATM | minibank (m) | ['mini,bɑnk] |

check	sjekk (m)	['ʂɛk]
to write a check	å skrive en sjekk	[ɔ 'skrivə en 'ʂɛk]
checkbook	sjekkbok (m/f)	['ʂɛk,bʊk]

loan (bank ~)	lån (n)	['lɔn]
to apply for a loan	å søke om lån	[ɔ ,søkə ɔm 'lɔn]
to get a loan	å få lån	[ɔ 'fɔ 'lɔn]
to give a loan	å gi lån	[ɔ 'ji 'lɔn]
guarantee	garanti (m)	[gɑran'ti]

44. Telephone. Phone conversation

telephone	telefon (m)	[tele'fʉn]
cell phone	mobiltelefon (m)	[mʉ'bil tele'fʉn]
answering machine	telefonsvarer (m)	[tele'fʉn‚svarər]
to call (by phone)	å ringe	[ɔ 'riŋə]
phone call	telefonsamtale (m)	[tele'fʉn 'sam‚talə]
to dial a number	å slå et nummer	[ɔ 'ʂlɔ et 'nʉmər]
Hello!	Hallo!	[ha'lʉ]
to ask (vt)	å spørre	[ɔ 'spørə]
to answer (vi, vt)	å svare	[ɔ 'svarə]
to hear (vt)	å høre	[ɔ 'hørə]
well (adv)	godt	['gɔt]
not well (adv)	dårlig	['doːli]
noises (interference)	støy (m)	['støj]
receiver	telefonrør (n)	[tele'fʉn‚rør]
to pick up (~ the phone)	å ta telefonen	[ɔ 'ta tele'fʉnən]
to hang up (~ the phone)	å legge på røret	[ɔ 'legə pɔ 'rørə]
busy (engaged)	opptatt	['ɔp‚tat]
to ring (ab. phone)	å ringe	[ɔ 'riŋə]
telephone book	telefonkatalog (m)	[tele'fʉn kata'lɔg]
local (adj)	lokal-	[lɔ'kal-]
local call	lokalsamtale (m)	[lɔ'kal 'sam‚talə]
long distance (~ call)	riks-	['riks-]
long-distance call	rikssamtale (m)	['riks 'sam‚talə]
international (adj)	internasjonal	['intɛ:ɳaʂʉ‚nal]
international call	internasjonal samtale (m)	['intɛ:ɳaʂʉ‚nal 'sam‚talə]

45. Cell phone

cell phone	mobiltelefon (m)	[mʉ'bil tele'fʉn]
display	skjerm (m)	['ʂærm]
button	knapp (m)	['knap]
SIM card	SIM-kort (n)	['sim‚kɔːt]
battery	batteri (n)	[batɛ'ri]
to be dead (battery)	å bli utladet	[ɔ 'bli 'ʉt‚ladət]
charger	lader (m)	['ladər]
menu	meny (m)	[me'ny]
settings	innstillinger (m/f pl)	['in‚stiliŋər]
tune (melody)	melodi (m)	[melɔ'di]
to select (vt)	å velge	[ɔ 'vɛlgə]

calculator	regnemaskin (m)	['rɛjnə maˌʂin]
voice mail	telefonsvarer (m)	[tele'funˌsvarər]
alarm clock	vekkerklokka (m/f)	['vɛkərˌklɔka]
contacts	kontakter (m pl)	[kʊn'taktər]

| SMS (text message) | SMS-beskjed (m) | [ɛsɛm'ɛs bɛˌʂɛ] |
| subscriber | abonnent (m) | [abɔ'nɛnt] |

46. Stationery

| ballpoint pen | kulepenn (m) | ['kʉːləˌpɛn] |
| fountain pen | fyllepenn (m) | ['fʏləˌpɛn] |

pencil	blyant (m)	['blyˌant]
highlighter	merkepenn (m)	['mærkəˌpɛn]
felt-tip pen	tusjpenn (m)	['tʉʂˌpɛn]

| notepad | notatbok (m/f) | [nʊ'tatˌbʊk] |
| agenda (diary) | dagbok (m/f) | ['dɑgˌbʊk] |

ruler	linjal (m)	[li'njɑl]
calculator	regnemaskin (m)	['rɛjnə maˌʂin]
eraser	viskelær (n)	['viskəˌlær]
thumbtack	tegnestift (m)	['tæjnəˌstift]
paper clip	binders (m)	['bindɛʂ]

glue	lim (n)	['lim]
stapler	stiftemaskin (m)	['stiftə maˌʂin]
hole punch	hullemaskin (m)	['hʉlə maˌʂin]
pencil sharpener	blyantspisser (m)	['blyantˌspisər]

47. Foreign languages

language	språk (n)	['sprɔk]
foreign (adj)	fremmed-	['freməˌ]
foreign language	fremmedspråk (n)	['fremedˌsprɔk]
to study (vt)	å studere	[ɔ stʉ'derə]
to learn (language, etc.)	å lære	[ɔ 'lærə]

to read (vi, vt)	å lese	[ɔ 'lesə]
to speak (vi, vt)	å tale	[ɔ 'talə]
to understand (vt)	å forstå	[ɔ fɔ'stɔ]
to write (vt)	å skrive	[ɔ 'skrivə]

fast (adv)	fort	['fuːt]
slowly (adv)	langsomt	['lɑŋsɔmt]
fluently (adv)	flytende	['flytnə]
rules	regler (m pl)	['rɛglər]

grammar	grammatikk (m)	[grɑmɑ'tik]
vocabulary	ordforråd (n)	['uːrfʊˌrɔd]
phonetics	fonetikk (m)	[fʊne'tik]

textbook	lærebok (m/f)	['læreˌbʊk]
dictionary	ordbok (m/f)	['uːrˌbʊk]
teach-yourself book	lærebok (m/f) for selvstudium	['læreˌbʊk fɔ 'selˌstʉdium]
phrasebook	parlør (m)	[pɑːˈlør]

cassette, tape	kassett (m)	[kɑ'sɛt]
videotape	videokassett (m)	['videʊ kɑ'sɛt]
CD, compact disc	CD-rom (m)	['sɛdɛˌrʊm]
DVD	DVD (m)	[deve'de]

alphabet	alfabet (n)	[ɑlfɑ'bet]
to spell (vt)	å stave	[ɔ 'stɑve]
pronunciation	uttale (m)	['ʉtˌtɑle]

accent	aksent (m)	[ɑk'sɑŋ]
with an accent	med aksent	[me ɑk'sɑŋ]
without an accent	uten aksent	['ʉten ɑk'sɑŋ]

| word | ord (n) | ['uːr] |
| meaning | betydning (m) | [be'tʏdniŋ] |

course (e.g., a French ~)	kurs (n)	['kʉʂ]
to sign up	å anmelde seg	[ɔ 'ɑnˌmɛle sæj]
teacher	lærer (m)	['lærer]

translation (process)	oversettelse (m)	['ɔveˌʂɛtelse]
translation (text, etc.)	oversettelse (m)	['ɔveˌʂɛtelse]
translator	oversetter (m)	['ɔveˌʂɛter]
interpreter	tolk (m)	['tɔlk]

| polyglot | polyglott (m) | [pʊlʏ'glɔt] |
| memory | minne (n),
hukommelse (m) | ['mine],
[hʉ'kɔmelse] |

MEALS. RESTAURANT

48. Table setting

spoon	skje (m)	['ʂe]
knife	kniv (m)	['kniv]
fork	gaffel (m)	['gafəl]
cup (e.g., coffee ~)	kopp (m)	['kɔp]
plate (dinner ~)	tallerken (m)	[ta'lærkən]
saucer	tefat (n)	['te͵fat]
napkin (on table)	serviett (m)	[sɛrvi'ɛt]
toothpick	tannpirker (m)	['tan͵pirkər]

49. Restaurant

restaurant	restaurant (m)	[rɛstʊ'raŋ]
coffee house	kafé, kaffebar (m)	[ka'fe], ['kafə͵bar]
pub, bar	bar (m)	['bar]
tearoom	tesalong (m)	['tesa͵lɔŋ]
waiter	servitør (m)	['særvi'tør]
waitress	servitrise (m/f)	[særvi'trisə]
bartender	bartender (m)	['baː͵tɛndər]
menu	meny (m)	[me'ny]
wine list	vinkart (n)	['vin͵kaːʈ]
to book a table	å reservere bord	[ɔ resɛr'verə 'bʊr]
course, dish	rett (m)	['rɛt]
to order (meal)	å bestille	[ɔ be'stilə]
to make an order	å bestille	[ɔ be'stilə]
aperitif	aperitiff (m)	[aperi'tif]
appetizer	forrett (m)	['fɔrɛt]
dessert	dessert (m)	[de'sɛːr]
check	regning (m/f)	['rɛjniŋ]
to pay the check	å betale regningen	[ɔ be'talə 'rɛjniŋən]
to give change	å gi tilbake veksel	[ɔ ji til'bakə 'vɛksəl]
tip	driks (m)	['driks]

50. Meals

food	mat (m)	['mat]
to eat (vi, vt)	å spise	[ɔ 'spisə]
breakfast	frokost (m)	['frʊkɔst]
to have breakfast	å spise frokost	[ɔ 'spisə ˌfrʊkɔst]
lunch	lunsj, lunch (m)	['lʉnʂ]
to have lunch	å spise lunsj	[ɔ 'spisə ˌlʉnʂ]
dinner	middag (m)	['miˌda]
to have dinner	å spise middag	[ɔ 'spisə 'miˌda]
appetite	appetitt (m)	[ape'tit]
Enjoy your meal!	God appetitt!	['gʊ ape'tit]
to open (~ a bottle)	å åpne	[ɔ 'ɔpnə]
to spill (liquid)	å spille	[ɔ 'spilə]
to spill out (vi)	å bli spilt	[ɔ 'bli 'spilt]
to boil (vi)	å koke	[ɔ 'kʊkə]
to boil (vt)	å koke	[ɔ 'kʊkə]
boiled (~ water)	kokt	['kʊkt]
to chill, cool down (vt)	å svalne	[ɔ 'svalnə]
to chill (vi)	å avkjøles	[ɔ 'avˌçœləs]
taste, flavor	smak (m)	['smak]
aftertaste	bismak (m)	['bismak]
to slim down (lose weight)	å være på diet	[ɔ 'værə pɔ di'et]
diet	diett (m)	[di'et]
vitamin	vitamin (n)	[vita'min]
calorie	kalori (m)	[kalʊ'ri]
vegetarian (n)	vegetarianer (m)	[vegetari'anər]
vegetarian (adj)	vegetarisk	[vege'tarisk]
fats (nutrient)	fett (n)	['fɛt]
proteins	proteiner (n pl)	[prɔte'inər]
carbohydrates	kullhydrater (n pl)	['kʉlhyˌdratər]
slice (of lemon, ham)	skive (m/f)	['ʂivə]
piece (of cake, pie)	stykke (n)	['stʏkə]
crumb	smule (m)	['smʉlə]
(of bread, cake, etc.)		

51. Cooked dishes

course, dish	rett (m)	['rɛt]
cuisine	kjøkken (n)	['çœkən]
recipe	oppskrift (m)	['ɔpˌskrift]
portion	porsjon (m)	[pɔ'ʂʊn]

| salad | salat (m) | [sɑ'lɑt] |
| soup | suppe (m/f) | ['sʉpə] |

clear soup (broth)	buljong (m)	[bu'ljɔŋ]
sandwich (bread)	smørbrød (n)	['smør,brø]
fried eggs	speilegg (n)	['spæjl,ɛg]

| hamburger (beefburger) | hamburger (m) | ['hambʉrgər] |
| beefsteak | biff (m) | ['bif] |

side dish	tilbehør (n)	['tilbə,hør]
spaghetti	spagetti (m)	[spɑ'gɛti]
mashed potatoes	potetmos (m)	[pʉ'tet,mʉs]
pizza	pizza (m)	['pitsɑ]
porridge (oatmeal, etc.)	grøt (m)	['grøt]
omelet	omelett (m)	[ɔmə'let]

boiled (e.g., ~ beef)	kokt	['kʉkt]
smoked (adj)	røkt	['røkt]
fried (adj)	stekt	['stɛkt]
dried (adj)	tørket	['tœrkət]
frozen (adj)	frossen, dypfryst	['frɔsən], ['dyp,frʏst]
pickled (adj)	syltet	['sʏltət]

sweet (sugary)	søt	['søt]
salty (adj)	salt	['sɑlt]
cold (adj)	kald	['kɑl]
hot (adj)	het, varm	['het], ['vɑrm]
bitter (adj)	bitter	['bitər]
tasty (adj)	lekker	['lekər]

to cook in boiling water	å koke	[ɔ 'kʉkə]
to cook (dinner)	å lage	[ɔ 'lɑgə]
to fry (vt)	å steke	[ɔ 'stekə]
to heat up (food)	å varme opp	[ɔ 'vɑrmə ɔp]

to salt (vt)	å salte	[ɔ 'sɑltə]
to pepper (vt)	å pepre	[ɔ 'pɛprə]
to grate (vt)	å rive	[ɔ 'rivə]
peel (n)	skall (n)	['skɑl]
to peel (vt)	å skrelle	[ɔ 'skrɛlə]

52. Food

meat	kjøtt (n)	['çœt]
chicken	høne (m/f)	['hønə]
Rock Cornish hen (poussin)	kylling (m)	['çyliŋ]
duck	and (m/f)	['ɑn]
goose	gås (m/f)	['gɔs]

| game | vilt (n) | ['vilt] |
| turkey | kalkun (m) | [kɑl'kʉn] |

pork	svinekjøtt (n)	['svinə,çœt]
veal	kalvekjøtt (n)	['kɑlvə,çœt]
lamb	fårekjøtt (n)	['foːrə,çœt]
beef	oksekjøtt (n)	['ɔksə,çœt]
rabbit	kanin (m)	[kɑ'nin]

sausage (bologna, pepperoni, etc.)	pølse (m/f)	['pølsə]
vienna sausage (frankfurter)	wienerpølse (m/f)	['vinər,pølsə]
bacon	bacon (n)	['bɛjkən]
ham	skinke (m)	['ʂinkə]
gammon	skinke (m)	['ʂinkə]

pâté	pate, paté (m)	[pɑ'te]
liver	lever (m)	['levər]
hamburger (ground beef)	kjøttfarse (m)	['çœt,fɑrʂə]
tongue	tunge (m/f)	['tʉŋə]

egg	egg (n)	['ɛg]
eggs	egg (n pl)	['ɛg]
egg white	eggehvite (m)	['ɛgə,vitə]
egg yolk	plomme (m/f)	['plʊmə]

fish	fisk (m)	['fisk]
seafood	sjømat (m)	['ʂøˌmɑt]
crustaceans	krepsdyr (n pl)	['krɛps,dyr]
caviar	kaviar (m)	['kɑviˌɑr]

crab	krabbe (m)	['krɑbə]
shrimp	reke (m/f)	['rekə]
oyster	østers (m)	['østəʂ]
spiny lobster	langust (m)	[lɑŋ'gʉst]
octopus	blekksprut (m)	['blek,sprʉt]
squid	blekksprut (m)	['blek,sprʉt]

sturgeon	stør (m)	['stør]
salmon	laks (m)	['lɑks]
halibut	kveite (m/f)	['kvæjtə]

cod	torsk (m)	['tɔʂk]
mackerel	makrell (m)	[mɑ'krɛl]
tuna	tunfisk (m)	['tʉn,fisk]
eel	ål (m)	['ɔl]

trout	ørret (m)	['øret]
sardine	sardin (m)	[sɑː'din]
pike	gjedde (m/f)	['jɛdə]
herring	sild (m/f)	['sil]

bread	brød (n)	['brø]
cheese	ost (m)	['ʊst]
sugar	sukker (n)	['sʉkər]
salt	salt (n)	['salt]

rice	ris (m)	['ris]
pasta (macaroni)	pasta, makaroni (m)	['pɑsta], [maka'rʊni]
noodles	nudler (m pl)	['nʉdlər]

butter	smør (n)	['smør]
vegetable oil	vegetabilsk olje (m)	[vegeta'bilsk ˌɔljə]
sunflower oil	solsikkeolje (m)	['sʊlsikəˌɔljə]
margarine	margarin (m)	[marga'rin]

| olives | olivener (m pl) | [ʊ'livenər] |
| olive oil | olivenolje (m) | [ʊ'livənˌɔljə] |

milk	melk (m/f)	['mɛlk]
condensed milk	kondensert melk (m/f)	[kʊndən'se:t ˌmɛlk]
yogurt	jogurt (m)	['jɔgʉ:t]
sour cream	rømme, syrnet fløte (m)	['rœmə], ['sy:ɳet 'fløtə]
cream (of milk)	fløte (m)	['fløtə]

| mayonnaise | majones (m) | [majo'nɛs] |
| buttercream | krem (m) | ['krɛm] |

cereal grains (wheat, etc.)	gryn (n)	['gryn]
flour	mel (n)	['mel]
canned food	hermetikk (m)	[hɛrme'tik]

cornflakes	cornflakes (m)	['kɔ:ɳˌflejks]
honey	honning (m)	['hɔniŋ]
jam	syltetøy (n)	['syltəˌtøj]
chewing gum	tyggegummi (m)	['tygəˌgʉmi]

53. Drinks

water	vann (n)	['van]
drinking water	drikkevann (n)	['drikəˌvan]
mineral water	mineralvann (n)	[minə'ralˌvan]

still (adj)	uten kullsyre	['ʉtən kʉl'syrə]
carbonated (adj)	kullsyret	[kʉl'syrət]
sparkling (adj)	med kullsyre	[me kʉl'syrə]
ice	is (m)	['is]
with ice	med is	[me 'is]

non-alcoholic (adj)	alkoholfri	['alkʊhʊlˌfri]
soft drink	alkoholfri drikk (m)	['alkʊhʊlˌfri drik]
refreshing drink	leskedrikk (m)	['leskəˌdrik]

lemonade	limonade (m)	[limɔ'nɑdə]
liquors	rusdrikker (m pl)	['rʉsˌdrikər]
wine	vin (m)	['vin]
white wine	hvitvin (m)	['vitˌvin]
red wine	rødvin (m)	['røˌvin]

liqueur	likør (m)	[li'kør]
champagne	champagne (m)	[ʂam'panjə]
vermouth	vermut (m)	['værmʉt]

whiskey	whisky (m)	['viski]
vodka	vodka (m)	['vɔdkɑ]
gin	gin (m)	['dʒin]
cognac	konjakk (m)	['kʊnjak]
rum	rom (m)	['rʊm]

coffee	kaffe (m)	['kɑfə]
black coffee	svart kaffe (m)	['svɑːʈ 'kɑfə]
coffee with milk	kaffe (m) med melk	['kɑfə me 'mɛlk]
cappuccino	cappuccino (m)	[kapʊ'tʃinɔ]
instant coffee	pulverkaffe (m)	['pʉlvərˌkɑfə]

milk	melk (m/f)	['mɛlk]
cocktail	cocktail (m)	['kɔkˌtɛjl]
milkshake	milkshake (m)	['milkˌʂɛjk]

juice	jus, juice (m)	['dʒʉs]
tomato juice	tomatjuice (m)	[tʊ'mɑtˌdʒʉs]
orange juice	appelsinjuice (m)	[apel'sinˌdʒʉs]
freshly squeezed juice	nypresset juice (m)	['nyˌprɛsə 'dʒʉs]

beer	øl (m/n)	['øl]
light beer	lettøl (n)	['letˌøl]
dark beer	mørkt øl (n)	['mœrktˌøl]

tea	te (m)	['te]
black tea	svart te (m)	['svɑːʈ ˌte]
green tea	grønn te (m)	['grœn ˌte]

54. Vegetables

| vegetables | grønnsaker (m pl) | ['grœnˌsɑkər] |
| greens | grønnsaker (m pl) | ['grœnˌsɑkər] |

tomato	tomat (m)	[tʊ'mɑt]
cucumber	agurk (m)	[a'gʉrk]
carrot	gulrot (m/f)	['gʉlˌrʊt]
potato	potet (m/f)	[pʊ'tet]
onion	løk (m)	['løk]
garlic	hvitløk (m)	['vitˌløk]

cabbage	kål (m)	['kɔl]
cauliflower	blomkål (m)	['blɔmˌkɔl]
Brussels sprouts	rosenkål (m)	['rʊsənˌkɔl]
broccoli	brokkoli (m)	['brɔkɔli]

beetroot	rødbete (m/f)	['røˌbetə]
eggplant	aubergine (m)	[ɔbɛr'ʂin]
zucchini	squash (m)	['skvɔʂ]
pumpkin	gresskar (n)	['grɛskɑr]
turnip	nepe (m/f)	['nepə]

parsley	persille (m/f)	[pæ'ʂilə]
dill	dill (m)	['dil]
lettuce	salat (m)	[sɑ'lɑt]
celery	selleri (m/n)	[sɛleˌri]
asparagus	asparges (m)	[ɑ'spɑrʂəs]
spinach	spinat (m)	[spi'nɑt]

pea	erter (m pl)	['æːʈər]
beans	bønner (m/f pl)	['bœnər]
corn (maize)	mais (m)	['mɑis]
kidney bean	bønne (m/f)	['bœnə]

bell pepper	pepper (m)	['pɛpər]
radish	reddik (m)	['rɛdik]
artichoke	artisjokk (m)	[ˌɑːʈi'ʂɔk]

55. Fruits. Nuts

fruit	frukt (m/f)	['frʉkt]
apple	eple (n)	['ɛplə]
pear	pære (m/f)	['pærə]
lemon	sitron (m)	[si'trʊn]
orange	appelsin (m)	[ɑpel'sin]
strawberry (garden ~)	jordbær (n)	['juːrˌbær]

mandarin	mandarin (m)	[mɑndɑ'rin]
plum	plomme (m/f)	['plʊmə]
peach	fersken (m)	['fæʂkən]
apricot	aprikos (m)	[ɑpri'kʊs]
raspberry	bringebær (n)	['briŋəˌbær]
pineapple	ananas (m)	['ɑnɑnɑs]

banana	banan (m)	[bɑ'nɑn]
watermelon	vannmelon (m)	['vɑnmeˌlʊn]
grape	drue (m)	['drʉə]
sour cherry	kirsebær (n)	['çiʂəˌbær]
sweet cherry	morell (m)	[mʊ'rɛl]
melon	melon (m)	[me'lun]
grapefruit	grapefrukt (m/f)	['grɛjpˌfrʉkt]

avocado	avokado (m)	[avɔ'kadɔ]
papaya	papaya (m)	[pa'paja]
mango	mango (m)	['maŋu]
pomegranate	granateple (n)	[gra'nat‚ɛplə]

redcurrant	rips (m)	['rips]
blackcurrant	solbær (n)	['sʊl‚bær]
gooseberry	stikkelsbær (n)	['stikəls‚bær]
bilberry	blåbær (n)	['blɔ‚bær]
blackberry	bjørnebær (m)	['bjœːŋə‚bær]

raisin	rosin (m)	[rʊ'sin]
fig	fiken (m)	['fikən]
date	daddel (m)	['dadəl]

peanut	jordnøtt (m)	['juːr‚nœt]
almond	mandel (m)	['mandəl]
walnut	valnøtt (m/f)	['val‚nœt]
hazelnut	hasselnøtt (m/f)	['hasəl‚nœt]
coconut	kokosnøtt (m/f)	['kʊkʊs‚nœt]
pistachios	pistasier (m pl)	[pi'staʂiər]

56. Bread. Candy

bakers' confectionery (pastry)	bakevarer (m/f pl)	['bakə‚varər]
bread	brød (n)	['brø]
cookies	kjeks (m)	['çɛks]

chocolate (n)	sjokolade (m)	[ʂʊkʊ'ladə]
chocolate (as adj)	sjokolade-	[ʂʊkʊ'ladə-]
candy (wrapped)	sukkertøy (n), karamell (m)	['sʉkəːtøj], [kara'mɛl]
cake (e.g., cupcake)	kake (m/f)	['kakə]
cake (e.g., birthday ~)	bløtkake (m/f)	['bløt‚kakə]

| pie (e.g., apple ~) | pai (m) | ['paj] |
| filling (for cake, pie) | fyll (m/n) | ['fʏl] |

jam (whole fruit jam)	syltetøy (n)	['syltə‚tøj]
marmalade	marmelade (m)	[marme'ladə]
waffles	vaffel (m)	['vafəl]
ice-cream	iskrem (m)	['iskrɛm]
pudding	pudding (m)	['pʉdiŋ]

57. Spices

| salt | salt (n) | ['salt] |
| salty (adj) | salt | ['salt] |

to salt (vt)	**å salte**	[ɔ 'saltə]
black pepper	**svart pepper** (m)	['svɑːʈ 'pɛpər]
red pepper (milled ~)	**rød pepper** (m)	['rø 'pɛpər]
mustard	**sennep** (m)	['sɛnəp]
horseradish	**pepperrot** (m/f)	['pɛpər‚rʊt]
condiment	**krydder** (n)	['krʏdər]
spice	**krydder** (n)	['krʏdər]
sauce	**saus** (m)	['saʊs]
vinegar	**eddik** (m)	['ɛdik]
anise	**anis** (m)	['ɑnis]
basil	**basilik** (m)	[bɑsi'lik]
cloves	**nellik** (m)	['nɛlik]
ginger	**ingefær** (m)	['iŋə‚fær]
coriander	**koriander** (m)	[kʊri'ɑndər]
cinnamon	**kanel** (m)	[kɑ'nel]
sesame	**sesam** (m)	['sesam]
bay leaf	**laurbærblad** (n)	['laʊrbær‚blɑ]
paprika	**paprika** (m)	['pɑprikɑ]
caraway	**karve, kummin** (m)	['kɑrvə], ['kʉmin]
saffron	**safran** (m)	[sɑ'frɑn]

PERSONAL INFORMATION. FAMILY

58. Personal information. Forms

name (first name)	navn (n)	['nɑvn]
surname (last name)	etternavn (n)	['ɛtə,nɑvn]
date of birth	fødselsdato (m)	['føtsəls,dɑtʊ]
place of birth	fødested (n)	['fødə,sted]
nationality	nasjonalitet (m)	[nɑsʊnɑli'tet]
place of residence	bosted (n)	['bʊ,sted]
country	land (n)	['lɑn]
profession (occupation)	yrke (n), profesjon (m)	['yrkə], [prʊfe'sʊn]
gender, sex	kjønn (n)	['çœn]
height	høyde (m)	['højdə]
weight	vekt (m)	['vɛkt]

59. Family members. Relatives

mother	mor (m/f)	['mʊr]
father	far (m)	['fɑr]
son	sønn (m)	['sœn]
daughter	datter (m/f)	['dɑtər]
younger daughter	yngste datter (m/f)	['yŋstə 'dɑtər]
younger son	yngste sønn (m)	['yŋstə 'sœn]
eldest daughter	eldste datter (m/f)	['ɛlstə 'dɑtər]
eldest son	eldste sønn (m)	['ɛlstə 'sœn]
brother	bror (m)	['brʊr]
elder brother	eldre bror (m)	['ɛldrə ,brʊr]
younger brother	lillebror (m)	['lilə,brʊr]
sister	søster (m/f)	['søstər]
elder sister	eldre søster (m/f)	['ɛldrə ,søstər]
younger sister	lillesøster (m/f)	['lilə,søstər]
cousin (masc.)	fetter (m/f)	['fɛtər]
cousin (fem.)	kusine (m)	[kʉ'sinə]
mom, mommy	mamma (m)	['mɑmɑ]
dad, daddy	pappa (m)	['pɑpɑ]
parents	foreldre (pl)	[fɔr'ɛldrə]
child	barn (n)	['bɑ:ɳ]
children	barn (n pl)	['bɑ:ɳ]

grandmother	**bestemor** (m)	['bɛstə‚mʊr]
grandfather	**bestefar** (m)	['bɛstə‚far]
grandson	**barnebarn** (n)	['bɑːnə‚bɑːn]
granddaughter	**barnebarn** (n)	['bɑːnə‚bɑːn]
grandchildren	**barnebarn** (n pl)	['bɑːnə‚bɑːn]

uncle	**onkel** (m)	['ʊnkəl]
aunt	**tante** (m/f)	['tɑntə]
nephew	**nevø** (m)	[ne'vø]
niece	**niese** (m/f)	[ni'esə]

mother-in-law (wife's mother)	**svigermor** (m/f)	['svigər‚mʊr]
father-in-law (husband's father)	**svigerfar** (m)	['svigər‚far]
son-in-law (daughter's husband)	**svigersønn** (m)	['svigər‚sœn]
stepmother	**stemor** (m/f)	['ste‚mʊr]
stepfather	**stefar** (m)	['ste‚far]
infant	**brystbarn** (n)	['brʏst‚bɑːn]
baby (infant)	**spedbarn** (n)	['spe‚bɑːn]
little boy, kid	**lite barn** (n)	['litə 'bɑːn]

wife	**kone** (m/f)	['kʊnə]
husband	**mann** (m)	['mɑn]
spouse (husband)	**ektemann** (m)	['ɛktə‚mɑn]
spouse (wife)	**hustru** (m)	['hʉstrʉ]

married (masc.)	**gift**	['jift]
married (fem.)	**gift**	['jift]
single (unmarried)	**ugift**	[ʉ'jift]
bachelor	**ungkar** (m)	['ʉŋ‚kar]
divorced (masc.)	**fraskilt**	['frɑ‚silt]
widow	**enke** (m)	['ɛnkə]
widower	**enkemann** (m)	['ɛnkə‚mɑn]

relative	**slektning** (m)	['ʂlektniŋ]
close relative	**nær slektning** (m)	['nær 'ʂlektniŋ]
distant relative	**fjern slektning** (m)	['fjæːɳ 'ʂlektniŋ]
relatives	**slektninger** (m pl)	['ʂlektniŋər]

orphan (boy or girl)	**foreldreløst barn** (n)	[fɔr'ɛldrəløst ‚bɑːn]
guardian (of a minor)	**formynder** (m)	['fɔr‚mʏnər]
to adopt (a boy)	**å adoptere**	[ɔ adɔp'terə]
to adopt (a girl)	**å adoptere**	[ɔ adɔp'terə]

60. Friends. Coworkers

friend (masc.)	**venn** (m)	['vɛn]
friend (fem.)	**venninne** (m/f)	[vɛ'ninə]

| friendship | vennskap (n) | ['vɛnˌskɑp] |
| to be friends | å være venner | [ɔ 'værə 'vɛnər] |

buddy (masc.)	venn (m)	['vɛn]
buddy (fem.)	venninne (m/f)	[vɛ'ninə]
partner	partner (m)	['pɑːʈnər]

chief (boss)	sjef (m)	['ʂɛf]
superior (n)	overordnet (m)	['ɔvərˌɔrdnet]
owner, proprietor	eier (m)	['æjər]
subordinate (n)	underordnet (m)	['ʉnərˌɔrdnet]
colleague	kollega (m)	[kʉ'legɑ]

acquaintance (person)	bekjent (m)	[be'çɛnt]
fellow traveler	medpassasjer (m)	['meˌpɑsɑ'sɛr]
classmate	klassekamerat (m)	['klɑsəˌkɑmə'rɑːt]

neighbor (masc.)	nabo (m)	['nɑbʉ]
neighbor (fem.)	nabo (m)	['nɑbʉ]
neighbors	naboer (m pl)	['nɑbʉər]

HUMAN BODY. MEDICINE

61. Head

head	hode (n)	['huɖə]
face	ansikt (n)	['ɑnsikt]
nose	nese (m/f)	['nesə]
mouth	munn (m)	['mʉn]

eye	øye (n)	['øjə]
eyes	øyne (n pl)	['øjnə]
pupil	pupill (m)	[pʉ'pil]
eyebrow	øyenbryn (n)	['øjən,bryn]
eyelash	øyenvipp (m)	['øjən,vip]
eyelid	øyelokk (m)	['øjə,lɔk]

tongue	tunge (m/f)	['tʉŋə]
tooth	tann (m/f)	['tan]
lips	lepper (m/f pl)	['lepər]
cheekbones	kinnbein (n pl)	['çin,bæjn]
gum	tannkjøtt (n)	['tan,çœt]
palate	gane (m)	['gɑnə]

nostrils	nesebor (n pl)	['nesə,bʉr]
chin	hake (m/f)	['hɑkə]
jaw	kjeve (m)	['çɛvə]
cheek	kinn (n)	['çin]

forehead	panne (m/f)	['panə]
temple	tinning (m)	['tiniŋ]
ear	øre (n)	['ørə]
back of the head	bakhode (n)	['bak,hoɖə]
neck	hals (m)	['hɑls]
throat	strupe, hals (m)	['strʉpə], ['hɑls]

hair	hår (n pl)	['hɔr]
hairstyle	frisyre (m)	[fri'syrə]
haircut	hårfasong (m)	['hoːrfɑ,sɔŋ]
wig	parykk (m)	[pɑ'rʏk]

mustache	mustasje (m)	[mʉ'stɑʂə]
beard	skjegg (n)	['ʂɛg]
to have (a beard, etc.)	å ha	[ɔ 'ha]
braid	flette (m/f)	['fletə]
sideburns	bakkenbarter (pl)	['bɑkən,baːʈər]
red-haired (adj)	rødhåret	['rø,hoːrət]

73

gray (hair)	grå	['grɔ]
bald (adj)	skallet	['skɑlət]
bald patch	skallet flekk (m)	['skɑlət ˌflek]

| ponytail | hestehale (m) | ['hɛstəˌhɑlə] |
| bangs | pannelugg (m) | ['pɑnəˌlʉg] |

62. Human body

| hand | hånd (m/f) | ['hɔn] |
| arm | arm (m) | ['ɑrm] |

finger	finger (m)	['fiŋər]
toe	tå (m/f)	['tɔ]
thumb	tommel (m)	['tɔməl]
little finger	lillefinger (m)	['liləˌfiŋər]
nail	negl (m)	['nɛjl]

fist	knyttneve (m)	['knʏtˌnevə]
palm	håndflate (m/f)	['hɔnˌflɑtə]
wrist	håndledd (n)	['hɔnˌled]
forearm	underarm (m)	['ʉnərˌɑrm]
elbow	albue (m)	['ɑlˌbʉə]
shoulder	skulder (m)	['skʉldər]

leg	bein (n)	['bæjn]
foot	fot (m)	['fʊt]
knee	kne (n)	['knɛ]
calf (part of leg)	legg (m)	['leg]
hip	hofte (m)	['hɔftə]
heel	hæl (m)	['hæl]

body	kropp (m)	['krɔp]
stomach	mage (m)	['mɑgə]
chest	bryst (n)	['brʏst]
breast	bryst (n)	['brʏst]
flank	side (m/f)	['sidə]
back	rygg (m)	['rʏg]
lower back	korsrygg (m)	['kɔːʂˌrʏg]
waist	liv (n), midje (m/f)	['liv], ['midjə]

navel (belly button)	navle (m)	['nɑvlə]
buttocks	rumpeballer (m pl)	['rʉmpəˌbɑlər]
bottom	bak (m)	['bɑk]

beauty mark	føflekk (m)	['føˌflek]
birthmark	fødselsmerke (n)	['føtsəlsˌmærkə]
(café au lait spot)		

| tattoo | tatovering (m/f) | [tatʉ'vɛriŋ] |
| scar | arr (n) | ['ɑr] |

63. Diseases

sickness	sykdom (m)	['svk͵dɔm]
to be sick	å være syk	[ɔ 'væːrə 'syk]
health	helse (m/f)	['hɛlsə]

runny nose (coryza)	snue (m)	['snʉə]
tonsillitis	angina (m)	[an'ginɑ]
cold (illness)	forkjølelse (m)	[fɔr'çœləlsə]
to catch a cold	å forkjøle seg	[ɔ fɔr'çœlə sæj]

bronchitis	bronkitt (m)	[brɔn'kit]
pneumonia	lungebetennelse (m)	['lʉŋə be'tɛnəlsə]
flu, influenza	influensa (m)	[inflʉ'ɛnsɑ]

nearsighted (adj)	nærsynt	['næ͵synt]
farsighted (adj)	langsynt	['laŋsynt]
strabismus (crossed eyes)	skjeløydhet (m)	['ʂɛløjd͵het]
cross-eyed (adj)	skjeløyd	['ʂɛl͵øjd]
cataract	grå stær, katarakt (m)	['grɔ ͵stær], [katɑ'rɑkt]
glaucoma	glaukom (n)	[glaʉ'kɔm]

stroke	hjerneslag (n)	['jæːŋə͵slɑg]
heart attack	infarkt (n)	[in'fɑrkt]
myocardial infarction	myokardieinfarkt (n)	['miɔ'kɑrdiə in'fɑrkt]
paralysis	paralyse, lammelse (m)	['pɑrɑ'lysə], ['lɑməlsə]
to paralyze (vt)	å lamme	[ɔ 'lɑmə]

allergy	allergi (m)	[ɑlæːˈgi]
asthma	astma (m)	['ɑstmɑ]
diabetes	diabetes (m)	[diɑ'betəs]

toothache	tannpine (m/f)	['tɑn͵pinə]
caries	karies (m)	['kɑries]

diarrhea	diaré (m)	[diɑ'rɛ]
constipation	forstoppelse (m)	[fɔ'ʂtɔpəlsə]
stomach upset	magebesvær (m)	['mɑgə͵be'svær]
food poisoning	matforgiftning (m/f)	['mɑt͵fɔr'jiftniŋ]
to get food poisoning	å få matforgiftning	[ɔ 'fɔ mɑt͵fɔr'jiftniŋ]

arthritis	artritt (m)	[ɑːṭ'rit]
rickets	rakitt (m)	[rɑ'kit]
rheumatism	revmatisme (m)	[revmɑ'tismə]
atherosclerosis	arteriosklerose (m)	[ɑːˈṭeriʊskle͵rʊsə]

gastritis	magekatarr, gastritt (m)	['mɑgəkɑ͵tɑr], [͵gɑ'strit]
appendicitis	appendisitt (m)	[ɑpɛndi'sit]
cholecystitis	galleblærebetennelse (m)	['gɑlə͵blærə be'tɛnəlsə]
ulcer	magesår (n)	['mɑgə͵sɔr]
measles	meslinger (m pl)	['mɛs͵liŋər]

rubella (German measles)	**røde hunder** (m pl)	['røde 'hʉnər]
jaundice	**gulsott** (m/f)	['gʉl‚sʊt]
hepatitis	**hepatitt** (m)	[hepɑ'tit]

schizophrenia	**schizofreni** (m)	[ʂisʊfre'ni]
rabies (hydrophobia)	**rabies** (m)	['rɑbies]
neurosis	**nevrose** (m)	[nev'rʊsə]
concussion	**hjernerystelse** (m)	['jæ:ɳə‚rʏstəlsə]

cancer	**kreft, cancer** (m)	['krɛft], ['kɑnsər]
sclerosis	**sklerose** (m)	[skle'rʊsə]
multiple sclerosis	**multippel sklerose** (m)	[mʉl'tipəl skle'rʊsə]

alcoholism	**alkoholisme** (m)	[ɑlkʊhʊ'lismə]
alcoholic (n)	**alkoholiker** (m)	[ɑlkʊ'hʊlikər]
syphilis	**syfilis** (m)	['syfilis]
AIDS	**AIDS, aids** (m)	['ɛjds]

tumor	**svulst, tumor** (m)	['svʉlst], [tʉ'mʊr]
malignant (adj)	**ondartet, malign**	['ʊn‚ɑ:ʈət], [mɑ'lign]
benign (adj)	**godartet**	['gʊ‚ɑ:ʈət]

fever	**feber** (m)	['febər]
malaria	**malaria** (m)	[mɑ'lɑriɑ]
gangrene	**koldbrann** (m)	['kɔlbrɑn]
seasickness	**sjøsyke** (m)	['ʂø‚sykə]
epilepsy	**epilepsi** (m)	[ɛpilep'si]

epidemic	**epidemi** (m)	[ɛpide'mi]
typhus	**tyfus** (m)	['tyfʉs]
tuberculosis	**tuberkulose** (m)	[tubærkʉ'lɔsə]
cholera	**kolera** (m)	['kʊlerɑ]
plague (bubonic ~)	**pest** (m)	['pɛst]

64. Symptoms. Treatments. Part 1

symptom	**symptom** (n)	[sʏmp'tʊm]
temperature	**temperatur** (m)	[tɛmpərɑ'tʉr]
high temperature (fever)	**høy temperatur** (m)	['høj tɛmpərɑ'tʉr]
pulse	**puls** (m)	['pʉls]

dizziness (vertigo)	**svimmelhet** (m)	['sviməl‚het]
hot (adj)	**varm**	['vɑrm]
shivering	**skjelving** (m/f)	['ʂɛlviŋ]
pale (e.g., ~ face)	**blek**	['blek]

cough	**hoste** (m)	['hʊstə]
to cough (vi)	**å hoste**	[ɔ 'hʊstə]
to sneeze (vi)	**å nyse**	[ɔ 'nysə]
faint	**besvimelse** (m)	[bɛ'sviməlsə]

to faint (vi)	å besvime	[ɔ be'svimə]
bruise (hématome)	blåmerke (n)	['blɔˌmærkə]
bump (lump)	bule (m)	['bʉlə]
to bang (bump)	å slå seg	[ɔ 'slɔ sæj]
contusion (bruise)	blåmerke (n)	['blɔˌmærkə]
to get a bruise	å slå seg	[ɔ 'slɔ sæj]

to limp (vi)	å halte	[ɔ 'haltə]
dislocation	forvridning (m)	[for'vridniŋ]
to dislocate (vt)	å forvri	[ɔ for'vri]
fracture	brudd (n), fraktur (m)	['brʉd], [frak'tʉr]
to have a fracture	å få brudd	[ɔ 'fɔ 'brʉd]

cut (e.g., paper ~)	skjæresår (n)	['şæːrəˌsɔr]
to cut oneself	å skjære seg	[ɔ 'şæːrə sæj]
bleeding	blødning (m/f)	['blødniŋ]

| burn (injury) | brannsår (n) | ['branˌsɔr] |
| to get burned | å brenne seg | [ɔ 'brɛnə sæj] |

to prick (vt)	å stikke	[ɔ 'stikə]
to prick oneself	å stikke seg	[ɔ 'stikə sæj]
to injure (vt)	å skade	[ɔ 'skadə]
injury	skade (n)	['skadə]
wound	sår (n)	['sɔr]
trauma	traume (m)	['traʊmə]

to be delirious	å snakke i villelse	[ɔ 'snakə i 'viləlsə]
to stutter (vi)	å stamme	[ɔ 'stamə]
sunstroke	solstikk (n)	['sʊlˌstik]

65. Symptoms. Treatments. Part 2

| pain, ache | smerte (m) | ['smæːtə] |
| splinter (in foot, etc.) | flis (m/f) | ['flis] |

sweat (perspiration)	svette (m)	['svɛtə]
to sweat (perspire)	å svette	[ɔ 'svɛtə]
vomiting	oppkast (n)	['ɔpˌkast]
convulsions	kramper (m pl)	['krampər]

pregnant (adj)	gravid	[gra'vid]
to be born	å fødes	[ɔ 'fødə]
delivery, labor	fødsel (m)	['føtsəl]
to deliver (~ a baby)	å føde	[ɔ 'fødə]
abortion	abort (m)	[a'bɔːt]

breathing, respiration	åndedrett (n)	['ɔndəˌdrɛt]
in-breath (inhalation)	innånding (m/f)	['inˌɔniŋ]
out-breath (exhalation)	utånding (m/f)	['ʉtˌɔndiŋ]

| to exhale (breathe out) | å puste ut | [ɔ 'pʉstə ʉt] |
| to inhale (vi) | å ånde inn | [ɔ 'ɔŋdə ˌin] |

disabled person	handikappet person (m)	['handiˌkapət pæ'ʂʉn]
cripple	krøpling (m)	['krøpliŋ]
drug addict	narkoman (m)	[narkʉ'man]

deaf (adj)	døv	['døv]
mute (adj)	stum	['stʉm]
deaf mute (adj)	døvstum	['døfˌstʉm]

mad, insane (adj)	gal	['gal]
madman (demented person)	gal mann (m)	['gal ˌman]
madwoman	gal kvinne (m/f)	['gal ˌkvinə]
to go insane	å bli sinnssyk	[ɔ 'bli 'sinˌsyk]

gene	gen (m)	['gen]
immunity	immunitet (m)	[imʉni'tet]
hereditary (adj)	arvelig	['arvəli]
congenital (adj)	medfødt	['meːˌføt]

virus	virus (m)	['virʉs]
microbe	mikrobe (m)	[mi'krʉbə]
bacterium	bakterie (m)	[bak'teriə]
infection	infeksjon (m)	[infɛk'ʂʉn]

66. Symptoms. Treatments. Part 3

| hospital | sykehus (n) | ['sykəˌhʉs] |
| patient | pasient (m) | [pasi'ɛnt] |

diagnosis	diagnose (m)	[dia'gnʉsə]
cure	kur (m)	['kʉr]
medical treatment	behandling (m/f)	[be'handliŋ]
to get treatment	å bli behandlet	[ɔ 'bli be'handlət]
to treat (~ a patient)	å behandle	[ɔ be'handlə]
to nurse (look after)	å skjøtte	[ɔ 'ʂøtə]
care (nursing ~)	sykepleie (m/f)	['sykəˌplæjə]

operation, surgery	operasjon (m)	[ɔpəra'ʂʉn]
to bandage (head, limb)	å forbinde	[ɔ fɔr'binə]
bandaging	forbinding (m)	[fɔr'biniŋ]

vaccination	vaksinering (m/f)	[vaksi'neriŋ]
to vaccinate (vt)	å vaksinere	[ɔ vaksi'nerə]
injection, shot	injeksjon (m), sprøyte (m/f)	[injɛk'ʂʉn], ['sprøjtə]
to give an injection	å gi en sprøyte	[ɔ 'ji en 'sprøjtə]
attack	anfall (n)	['anˌfal]
amputation	amputasjon (m)	[ampʉta'ʂʉn]

to amputate (vt)	å amputere	[ɔ ampʉˈterə]
coma	koma (m)	[ˈkʊma]
to be in a coma	å ligge i koma	[ɔ ˈligə i ˈkʊma]
intensive care	intensivavdeling (m/f)	[ˈintenˌsiv ˈavˌdeliŋ]

to recover (~ from flu)	å bli frisk	[ɔ ˈbli ˈfrisk]
condition (patient's ~)	tilstand (m)	[ˈtilˌstan]
consciousness	bevissthet (m)	[beˈvistˌhet]
memory (faculty)	minne (n),	[ˈminə],
	hukommelse (m)	[hʉˈkɔməlsə]

to pull out (tooth)	å trekke ut	[ɔ ˈtrɛkə ʉt]
filling	fylling (m/f)	[ˈfʏliŋ]
to fill (a tooth)	å plombere	[ɔ plʊmˈberə]

| hypnosis | hypnose (m) | [hʏpˈnʊsə] |
| to hypnotize (vt) | å hypnotisere | [ɔ hʏpnʊtiˈserə] |

67. Medicine. Drugs. Accessories

medicine, drug	medisin (m)	[mediˈsin]
remedy	middel (n)	[ˈmidəl]
to prescribe (vt)	å ordinere	[ɔ ɔrdiˈnerə]
prescription	resept (m)	[reˈsɛpt]

tablet, pill	tablett (m)	[tabˈlet]
ointment	salve (m/f)	[ˈsalvə]
ampule	ampulle (m)	[amˈpʉlə]
mixture	mikstur (m)	[miksˈtʉr]
syrup	sirup (m)	[ˈsirʉp]
pill	pille (m/f)	[ˈpilə]
powder	pulver (n)	[ˈpʉlvər]

gauze bandage	gasbind (n)	[ˈgasˌbin]
cotton wool	vatt (m/n)	[ˈvat]
iodine	jod (m/n)	[ˈʉd]

Band-Aid	plaster (n)	[ˈplastər]
eyedropper	pipette (m)	[piˈpɛtə]
thermometer	termometer (n)	[tɛrmʊˈmetər]
syringe	sprøyte (m/f)	[ˈsprøjtə]

| wheelchair | rullestol (m) | [ˈrʉləˌstʊl] |
| crutches | krykker (m/f pl) | [ˈkrʏkər] |

painkiller	smertestillende middel (n)	[ˈsmæːˌtəˌstilenə ˈmidəl]
laxative	laksativ (n)	[laksaˈtiv]
spirits (ethanol)	sprit (m)	[ˈsprit]
medicinal herbs	legeurter (m/f pl)	[ˈlegəˌʉːtər]
herbal (~ tea)	urte-	[ˈʉːtə-]

APARTMENT

68. Apartment

apartment	leilighet (m/f)	['læjli,het]
room	rom (n)	['rʊm]
bedroom	soverom (n)	['sɔvə,rʊm]
dining room	spisestue (m/f)	['spisə,stʉə]
living room	dagligstue (m/f)	['dɑgli,stʉə]
study (home office)	arbeidsrom (n)	['ɑrbæjds,rʊm]
entry room	entré (m)	[ɑn'trɛ:]
bathroom (room with a bath or shower)	bad, baderom (n)	['bɑd], ['bɑdə,rʊm]
half bath	toalett, WC (n)	[tʊɑ'let], [vɛ'sɛ]
ceiling	tak (n)	['tɑk]
floor	gulv (n)	['gʉlv]
corner	hjørne (n)	['jœ:ŋə]

69. Furniture. Interior

furniture	møbler (n pl)	['møblər]
table	bord (n)	['bʊr]
chair	stol (m)	['stʊl]
bed	seng (m/f)	['sɛŋ]
couch, sofa	sofa (m)	['sʊfɑ]
armchair	lenestol (m)	['lenə,stʊl]
bookcase	bokskap (n)	['bʊk,skɑp]
shelf	hylle (m/f)	['hʏlə]
wardrobe	klesskap (n)	['kle,skɑp]
coat rack (wall-mounted ~)	knaggbrett (n)	['knɑg,brɛt]
coat stand	stumtjener (m)	['stʉm,tjenər]
bureau, dresser	kommode (m)	[kʊ'mʊdə]
coffee table	kaffebord (n)	['kɑfə,bʊr]
mirror	speil (n)	['spæjl]
carpet	teppe (n)	['tɛpə]
rug, small carpet	lite teppe (n)	['litə 'tɛpə]
fireplace	peis (m), ildsted (n)	['pæjs], ['ilsted]
candle	lys (n)	['lys]

candlestick	lysestake (m)	['lysəˌstɑkə]
drapes	gardiner (m/f pl)	[gɑːˈdinər]
wallpaper	tapet (n)	[tɑˈpet]
blinds (jalousie)	persienne (m)	[pæʂiˈenə]

table lamp	bordlampe (m/f)	['bʊrˌlɑmpə]
wall lamp (sconce)	vegglampe (m/f)	['vɛgˌlɑmpə]
floor lamp	gulvlampe (m/f)	['gʉlvˌlɑmpə]
chandelier	lysekrone (m/f)	['lysəˌkrʊnə]

leg (of chair, table)	bein (n)	['bæjn]
armrest	armlene (n)	['ɑrmˌlenə]
back (backrest)	rygg (m)	['rʏg]
drawer	skuff (m)	['skʉf]

70. Bedding

bedclothes	sengetøy (n)	['sɛŋəˌtøj]
pillow	pute (m/f)	['pʉtə]
pillowcase	putevar, putetrekk (n)	['pʉtəˌvɑr], ['pʉtəˌtrɛk]
duvet, comforter	dyne (m/f)	['dynə]
sheet	laken (n)	['lɑkən]
bedspread	sengeteppe (n)	['sɛŋəˌtɛpə]

71. Kitchen

kitchen	kjøkken (n)	['çœkən]
gas	gass (m)	['gɑs]
gas stove (range)	gasskomfyr (m)	['gɑs kɔmˌfyr]
electric stove	elektrisk komfyr (m)	[ɛˈlektrisk kɔmˌfyr]
oven	bakeovn (m)	['bɑkəˌɔvn]
microwave oven	mikrobølgeovn (m)	['mikrʊˌbølgəˈɔvn]

refrigerator	kjøleskap (n)	['çœləˌskɑp]
freezer	fryser (m)	['frysər]
dishwasher	oppvaskmaskin (m)	['ɔpvɑsk mɑˌʂin]

meat grinder	kjøttkvern (m/f)	['çœtˌkvɛːn]
juicer	juicepresse (m/f)	['dʒʉsˌprɛsə]
toaster	brødrister (m)	['brøˌristər]
mixer	mikser (m)	['miksər]

coffee machine	kaffetrakter (m)	['kɑfəˌtrɑktər]
coffee pot	kaffekanne (m/f)	['kɑfəˌkɑnə]
coffee grinder	kaffekvern (m/f)	['kɑfəˌkvɛːn]

| kettle | tekjele (m) | ['teˌçələ] |
| teapot | tekanne (m/f) | ['teˌkɑnə] |

| lid | lokk (n) | ['lɔk] |
| tea strainer | tesil (m) | ['teˌsil] |

spoon	skje (m)	['ʂe]
teaspoon	teskje (m)	['teˌʂe]
soup spoon	spiseskje (m)	['spisəˌʂɛ]
fork	gaffel (m)	['gafəl]
knife	kniv (m)	['kniv]

tableware (dishes)	servise (n)	[sær'visə]
plate (dinner ~)	tallerken (m)	[tɑ'lærkən]
saucer	tefat (n)	['teˌfɑt]

shot glass	shotglass (n)	['ʂɔtˌglɑs]
glass (tumbler)	glass (n)	['glɑs]
cup	kopp (m)	['kɔp]

sugar bowl	sukkerskål (m/f)	['sʉkərˌskɔl]
salt shaker	saltbøsse (m/f)	['sɑltˌbøsə]
pepper shaker	pepperbøsse (m/f)	['pɛpərˌbøsə]
butter dish	smørkopp (m)	['smœrˌkɔp]

stock pot (soup pot)	gryte (m/f)	['grytə]
frying pan (skillet)	steikepanne (m/f)	['stæjkəˌpɑnə]
ladle	sleiv (m/f)	['ʂlæjv]
colander	dørslag (n)	['dœʂlɑg]
tray (serving ~)	brett (n)	['brɛt]

bottle	flaske (m)	['flɑskə]
jar (glass)	glasskrukke (m/f)	['glɑsˌkrʉkə]
can	boks (m)	['bɔks]

bottle opener	flaskeåpner (m)	['flɑskəˌɔpnər]
can opener	konservåpner (m)	['kʉnsəvˌɔpnər]
corkscrew	korketrekker (m)	['kɔrkəˌtrɛkər]
filter	filter (n)	['filtər]
to filter (vt)	å filtrere	[ɔ fil'trerə]

| trash, garbage (food waste, etc.) | søppel (m/f/n) | ['sœpəl] |
| trash can (kitchen ~) | søppelbøtte (m/f) | ['sœpəlˌbœtə] |

72. Bathroom

bathroom	bad, baderom (n)	['bɑd], ['bɑdəˌrʊm]
water	vann (n)	['vɑn]
faucet	kran (m/f)	['krɑn]
hot water	varmt vann (n)	['vɑrmt ˌvɑn]
cold water	kaldt vann (n)	['kɑlt vɑn]
toothpaste	tannpasta (m)	['tɑnˌpɑstɑ]

| to brush one's teeth | å pusse tennene | [ɔ 'pʉsə 'tɛnənə] |
| toothbrush | tannbørste (m) | ['tɑn‚bœʂtə] |

to shave (vi)	å barbere seg	[ɔ bɑr'berə sæj]
shaving foam	barberskum (n)	[bɑr'bɛ‚skʉm]
razor	høvel (m)	['høvəl]

to wash (one's hands, etc.)	å vaske	[ɔ 'vɑskə]
to take a bath	å vaske seg	[ɔ 'vɑskə sæj]
shower	dusj (m)	['dʉʂ]
to take a shower	å ta en dusj	[ɔ 'tɑ en 'dʉʂ]

bathtub	badekar (n)	['bɑdə‚kɑr]
toilet (toilet bowl)	toalettstol (m)	[tʊɑ'let‚stʉl]
sink (washbasin)	vaskeservant (m)	['vɑskə‚sɛr'vɑnt]

| soap | såpe (m/f) | ['soːpə] |
| soap dish | såpeskål (m/f) | ['soːpə‚skɔl] |

sponge	svamp (m)	['svɑmp]
shampoo	sjampo (m)	['ʂɑm‚pʊ]
towel	håndkle (n)	['hɔn‚kle]
bathrobe	badekåpe (m/f)	['bɑdə‚koːpə]

laundry (process)	vask (m)	['vɑsk]
washing machine	vaskemaskin (m)	['vɑskə mɑ‚ʂin]
to do the laundry	å vaske tøy	[ɔ 'vɑskə 'tøj]
laundry detergent	vaskepulver (n)	['vɑskə‚pʉlvər]

73. Household appliances

TV set	TV (m), TV-apparat (n)	['tɛvɛ], ['tɛvɛ ɑpɑ'rɑt]
tape recorder	båndopptaker (m)	['bɔn‚ɔptɑkər]
VCR (video recorder)	video (m)	['videʊ]
radio	radio (m)	['rɑdiʊ]
player (CD, MP3, etc.)	spiller (m)	['spilər]

video projector	videoprojektor (m)	['videʊ prɔ'jɛktɔr]
home movie theater	hjemmekino (m)	['jɛmə‚çinʊ]
DVD player	DVD-spiller (m)	[deve'de ‚spilər]
amplifier	forsterker (m)	[fɔ'ʂtærkər]
video game console	spillkonsoll (m)	['spil kʊn'sɔl]

video camera	videokamera (n)	['videʊ ‚kɑmerɑ]
camera (photo)	kamera (n)	['kɑmerɑ]
digital camera	digitalkamera (n)	[digi'tɑl ‚kɑmerɑ]

vacuum cleaner	støvsuger (m)	['støf‚sʉgər]
iron (e.g., steam ~)	strykejern (n)	['strykə‚jæːn]
ironing board	strykebrett (n)	['strykə‚brɛt]

telephone	**telefon** (m)	[teleˈfʊn]
cell phone	**mobiltelefon** (m)	[mʊˈbil teleˈfʊn]
typewriter	**skrivemaskin** (m)	[ˈskrivə maˌʂin]
sewing machine	**symaskin** (m)	[ˈsiːmaˌʂin]

microphone	**mikrofon** (m)	[mikrʊˈfʊn]
headphones	**hodetelefoner** (n pl)	[ˈhɔdəteləˌfunər]
remote control (TV)	**fjernkontroll** (m)	[ˈfjæːn̩ kʊnˈtrɔl]

CD, compact disc	**CD-rom** (m)	[ˈsɛdɛˌrʊm]
cassette, tape	**kassett** (m)	[kaˈsɛt]
vinyl record	**plate, skive** (m/f)	[ˈplatə], [ˈʂivə]

THE EARTH. WEATHER

74. Outer space

space	rommet, kosmos (n)	['rʊmə], ['kɔsmɔs]
space (as adj)	rom-	['rʊm-]
outer space	ytre rom (n)	['ytrə ˌrʊm]
world	verden (m)	['værdən]
universe	univers (n)	[ʉni'væʂ]
galaxy	galakse (m)	[gɑ'lɑksə]
star	stjerne (m/f)	['stjæːŋə]
constellation	stjernebilde (n)	['stjæːŋəˌbildə]
planet	planet (m)	[plɑ'net]
satellite	satellitt (m)	[sɑtɛ'lit]
meteorite	meteoritt (m)	[meteʊ'rit]
comet	komet (m)	[kʊ'met]
asteroid	asteroide (n)	[ɑsterʊ'idə]
orbit	bane (m)	['bɑnə]
to revolve	å rotere	[ɔ rɔ'terə]
(~ around the Earth)		
atmosphere	atmosfære (m)	[ɑtmʊ'sfærə]
the Sun	Solen	['sʊlən]
solar system	solsystem (n)	['sʊl sʏ'stem]
solar eclipse	solformørkelse (m)	['sʊl fɔr'mœrkəlsə]
the Earth	Jorden	['juːrən]
the Moon	Månen	['moːnən]
Mars	Mars	['mɑʂ]
Venus	Venus	['venʉs]
Jupiter	Jupiter	['jʉpitər]
Saturn	Saturn	['sɑˌtʉːn]
Mercury	Merkur	[mær'kʉr]
Uranus	Uranus	[ʉ'rɑnʉs]
Neptune	Neptun	[nɛp'tʉn]
Pluto	Pluto	['plʉtʊ]
Milky Way	Melkeveien	['mɛlkəˌvæjən]
Great Bear (Ursa Major)	den Store Bjørn	['dən 'stʉrə ˌbjœːn]
North Star	Nordstjernen, Polaris	['nuːrˌstjæːnən], [pɔ'laris]
Martian	marsbeboer (m)	['mɑʂˌbebʉər]

extraterrestrial (n)	utenomjordisk vesen (n)	['ʉtənɔmˌjuːrdisk 'vesən]
alien	romvesen (n)	['rʊmˌvesən]
flying saucer	flygende tallerken (m)	['flygenə taˈlærkən]

spaceship	romskip (n)	['rʊmˌʂip]
space station	romstasjon (m)	['rʊmˌstaˈʂʊn]
blast-off	start (m), oppskyting (m/f)	['stɑːt], ['ɔpˌʂytiŋ]

engine	motor (m)	['mɔtʊr]
nozzle	dyse (m)	['dysə]
fuel	brensel (n), drivstoff (n)	['brɛnsəl], ['drifˌstɔf]

cockpit, flight deck	cockpit (m), flydekk (n)	['kɔkpit], ['flyˌdɛk]
antenna	antenne (m)	[anˈtɛnə]
porthole	koøye (n)	['kʊˌøjə]
solar panel	solbatteri (n)	['sʊl batɛˈri]
spacesuit	romdrakt (m/f)	['rʊmˌdrakt]

| weightlessness | vektløshet (m/f) | ['vɛktløsˌhet] |
| oxygen | oksygen (n) | ['ɔksyˈgen] |

| docking (in space) | dokking (m/f) | ['dɔkiŋ] |
| to dock (vi, vt) | å dokke | [ɔ 'dɔkə] |

observatory	observatorium (n)	[ɔbsərvaˈtʊrium]
telescope	teleskop (n)	[teleˈskʊp]
to observe (vt)	å observere	[ɔ ɔbsɛrˈverə]
to explore (vt)	å utforske	[ɔ 'ʉtˌfɔʂkə]

75. The Earth

the Earth	Jorden	['juːrən]
the globe (the Earth)	jordklode (m)	['juːrˌklodə]
planet	planet (m)	[plaˈnet]

atmosphere	atmosfære (m)	[atmʊˈsfærə]
geography	geografi (m)	[geʊgraˈfi]
nature	natur (m)	[naˈtʉr]

globe (table ~)	globus (m)	['globʉs]
map	kart (n)	['kɑːt]
atlas	atlas (n)	['atlas]

Europe	Europa	[ɛʉˈrʊpa]
Asia	Asia	['asia]
Africa	Afrika	['afrika]
Australia	Australia	[aʊ'strɑliɑ]

| America | Amerika | [aˈmerika] |
| North America | Nord-Amerika | ['nʊːr aˈmerika] |

South America	Sør-Amerika	['sør ɑ'merikɑ]
Antarctica	Antarktis	[ɑn'tɑrktis]
the Arctic	Arktis	['ɑrktis]

76. Cardinal directions

north	nord (n)	['nʊːr]
to the north	mot nord	[mʊt 'nʊːr]
in the north	i nord	[i 'nʊːr]
northern (adj)	nordlig	['nʊːrli]

south	syd, sør	['syd], ['sør]
to the south	mot sør	[mʊt 'sør]
in the south	i sør	[i 'sør]
southern (adj)	sydlig, sørlig	['sydli], ['søː[i]

west	vest (m)	['vɛst]
to the west	mot vest	[mʊt 'vɛst]
in the west	i vest	[i 'vɛst]
western (adj)	vestlig, vest-	['vɛstli]

east	øst (m)	['øst]
to the east	mot øst	[mʊt 'øst]
in the east	i øst	[i 'øst]
eastern (adj)	østlig	['østli]

77. Sea. Ocean

sea	hav (n)	['hɑv]
ocean	verdenshav (n)	[værdəns'hɑv]
gulf (bay)	bukt (m/f)	['bʉkt]
straits	sund (n)	['sʉn]

land (solid ground)	fastland (n)	['fɑst,lɑn]
continent (mainland)	fastland, kontinent (n)	['fɑst,lɑn], [kʊnti'nɛnt]
island	øy (m/f)	['øj]
peninsula	halvøy (m/f)	['hɑl,øːj]
archipelago	skjærgård (m), arkipelag (n)	['sær,gɔr], [ɑrkipe'lɑg]

bay, cove	bukt (m/f)	['bʉkt]
harbor	havn (m/f)	['hɑvn]
lagoon	lagune (m)	[lɑ'gʉnə]
cape	nes (n), kapp (n)	['nes], ['kɑp]

atoll	atoll (m)	[ɑ'tɔl]
reef	rev (n)	['rev]
coral	korall (m)	[kʊ'rɑl]

coral reef	**korallrev** (n)	[kʊ'ral,rɛv]
deep (adj)	**dyp**	['dyp]
depth (deep water)	**dybde** (m)	['dʏbdə]
abyss	**avgrunn** (m)	['av,grʉn]
trench (e.g., Mariana ~)	**dyphavsgrop** (m/f)	['dyphafs,grɔp]
current (Ocean ~)	**strøm** (m)	['strøm]
to surround (bathe)	**å omgi**	[ɔ 'ɔm,ji]
shore	**kyst** (m)	['çyst]
coast	**kyst** (m)	['çyst]
flow (flood tide)	**flo** (m/f)	['flʊ]
ebb (ebb tide)	**ebbe** (m), **fjære** (m/f)	['ɛbə], ['fjærə]
shoal	**sandbanke** (m)	['san,baŋkə]
bottom (~ of the sea)	**bunn** (m)	['bʉn]
wave	**bølge** (m)	['bølgə]
crest (~ of a wave)	**bølgekam** (m)	['bølgə,kam]
spume (sea foam)	**skum** (n)	['skʉm]
storm (sea storm)	**storm** (m)	['stɔrm]
hurricane	**orkan** (m)	[ɔr'kan]
tsunami	**tsunami** (m)	[tsʉ'nami]
calm (dead ~)	**stille** (m/f)	['stilə]
quiet, calm (adj)	**stille**	['stilə]
pole	**pol** (m)	['pʊl]
polar (adj)	**pol-, polar**	['pʊl-], [pʊ'lar]
latitude	**bredde, latitude** (m)	['brɛdə], ['lati,tʉdə]
longitude	**lengde** (m/f)	['leŋdə]
parallel	**breddegrad** (m)	['brɛdə,grad]
equator	**ekvator** (m)	[ɛ'kvatʊr]
sky	**himmel** (m)	['himəl]
horizon	**horisont** (m)	[hʊri'sɔnt]
air	**luft** (f)	['lʉft]
lighthouse	**fyr** (n)	['fyr]
to dive (vi)	**å dykke**	[ɔ 'dʏkə]
to sink (ab. boat)	**å synke**	[ɔ 'sʏnkə]
treasures	**skatter** (m pl)	['skatər]

78. Seas' and Oceans' names

Atlantic Ocean	**Atlanterhavet**	[at'lantər,havə]
Indian Ocean	**Indiahavet**	['india,havə]
Pacific Ocean	**Stillehavet**	['stilə,havə]
Arctic Ocean	**Polhavet**	['pɔl,havə]

Black Sea	Svartehavet	['svɑːtəˌhɑve]
Red Sea	Rødehavet	['rødəˌhɑve]
Yellow Sea	Gulehavet	['gɵləˌhɑve]
White Sea	Kvitsjøen, Hvitehavet	['kvitˌsøːn], ['vitˌhɑve]

Caspian Sea	Kaspihavet	['kɑspiˌhɑve]
Dead Sea	Dødehavet	['dødə'hɑve]
Mediterranean Sea	Middelhavet	['midəlˌhɑve]

| Aegean Sea | Egeerhavet | [ɛ'geːərˌhɑve] |
| Adriatic Sea | Adriahavet | ['ɑdriɑˌhɑve] |

Arabian Sea	Arabiahavet	[ɑ'rɑbiɑˌhɑve]
Sea of Japan	Japanhavet	['jɑpɑnˌhɑve]
Bering Sea	Beringhavet	['beriŋˌhɑve]
South China Sea	Sør-Kina-havet	['sørˌçinɑ 'hɑve]

Coral Sea	Korallhavet	[kʊ'rɑlˌhɑve]
Tasman Sea	Tasmanhavet	[tɑs'mɑnˌhɑve]
Caribbean Sea	Karibhavet	[kɑ'ribˌhɑve]

| Barents Sea | Barentshavet | ['bɑrɛnsˌhɑve] |
| Kara Sea | Karahavet | ['kɑrɑˌhɑve] |

North Sea	Nordsjøen	['nuːrˌsøːn]
Baltic Sea	Østersjøen	['østəˌsøːn]
Norwegian Sea	Norskehavet	['nɔʂkəˌhɑve]

79. Mountains

mountain	fjell (n)	['fjɛl]
mountain range	fjellkjede (m)	['fjɛlˌçɛːdə]
mountain ridge	fjellrygg (m)	['fjɛlˌrʏg]

summit, top	topp (m)	['tɔp]
peak	tind (m)	['tin]
foot (~ of the mountain)	fot (m)	['fʊt]
slope (mountainside)	skråning (m)	['skrɔniŋ]

volcano	vulkan (m)	[vɵl'kɑn]
active volcano	virksom vulkan (m)	['virksɔm vɵl'kɑn]
dormant volcano	utslukt vulkan (m)	['ɵtˌslɵkt vɵl'kɑn]

eruption	utbrudd (n)	['ɵtˌbrɵd]
crater	krater (n)	['krɑtər]
magma	magma (m/n)	['mɑgmɑ]
lava	lava (m)	['lɑvɑ]
molten (~ lava)	glødende	['glødenə]
canyon	canyon (m)	['kɑnjən]
gorge	gjel (n), kløft (m)	['jel], ['klœft]

crevice	renne (m/f)	['rɛnə]
abyss (chasm)	avgrunn (m)	['ɑvˌgrʉn]
pass, col	pass (n)	['pɑs]
plateau	platå (n)	[plɑ'to]
cliff	klippe (m)	['klipə]
hill	ås (m)	['ɔs]
glacier	bre, jøkel (m)	['bre], ['jøkəl]
waterfall	foss (m)	['fɔs]
geyser	geysir (m)	['gɛjsir]
lake	innsjø (m)	['in'ʂø]
plain	slette (m/f)	['ʂletə]
landscape	landskap (n)	['lɑnˌskɑp]
echo	ekko (n)	['ɛkʉ]
alpinist	alpinist (m)	[ɑlpi'nist]
rock climber	fjellklatrer (m)	['fjɛlˌklɑtrər]
to conquer (in climbing)	å erobre	[ɔ ɛ'rʉbrə]
climb (an easy ~)	bestigning (m/f)	[be'stigniŋ]

80. Mountains names

The Alps	Alpene	['ɑlpenə]
Mont Blanc	Mont Blanc	[ˌmɔn'blɑn]
The Pyrenees	Pyreneene	[pyre'ne:ənə]
The Carpathians	Karpatene	[kɑr'pɑtenə]
The Ural Mountains	Uralfjellene	[ʉ'rɑl ˌfjɛlenə]
The Caucasus Mountains	Kaukasus	['kaʉkɑsʉs]
Mount Elbrus	Elbrus	[ɛl'brʉs]
The Altai Mountains	Altaj	[ɑl'tɑj]
The Tian Shan	Tien Shan	[ti'enˌʂɑn]
The Pamir Mountains	Pamir	[pɑ'mir]
The Himalayas	Himalaya	[himɑ'lɑja]
Mount Everest	Everest	['ɛve'rɛst]
The Andes	Andes	['ɑndəs]
Mount Kilimanjaro	Kilimanjaro	[kilimɑn'dʂɑrʉ]

81. Rivers

river	elv (m/f)	['ɛlv]
spring (natural source)	kilde (m)	['çildə]
riverbed (river channel)	elveleie (n)	['ɛlvəˌlæje]
basin (river valley)	flodbasseng (n)	['flʉd bɑˌseŋ]

to flow into ...	å munne ut ...	[ɔ 'mʉnə ʉt ...]
tributary	bielv (m/f)	['biˌelv]
bank (of river)	bredd (m)	['brɛd]
current (stream)	strøm (m)	['strøm]
downstream (adv)	medstrøms	['meˌstrøms]
upstream (adv)	motstrøms	['mʉtˌstrøms]
inundation	oversvømmelse (m)	['ɔveˌsvœməlsə]
flooding	flom (m)	['flɔm]
to overflow (vi)	å overflø	[ɔ 'ɔvərˌflø]
to flood (vt)	å oversvømme	[ɔ 'ɔveˌsvœmə]
shallow (shoal)	grunne (m/f)	['grʉnə]
rapids	stryk (m/n)	['stryk]
dam	demning (m)	['dɛmniŋ]
canal	kanal (m)	[ka'nal]
reservoir (artificial lake)	reservoar (n)	[resɛrvʉ'ar]
sluice, lock	sluse (m)	['ʂlʉsə]
water body (pond, etc.)	vannmasse (m)	['vanˌmasə]
swamp (marshland)	myr, sump (m)	['myr], ['sʉmp]
bog, marsh	hengemyr (m)	['hɛŋeˌmyr]
whirlpool	virvel (m)	['virvəl]
stream (brook)	bekk (m)	['bɛk]
drinking (ab. water)	drikke-	['drikə-]
fresh (~ water)	fersk-	['fæʂk-]
ice	is (m)	['is]
to freeze over	å fryse til	[ɔ 'frysə til]
(ab. river, etc.)		

82. Rivers' names

Seine	Seine	['sɛːn]
Loire	Loire	[lu'aːr]
Thames	Themsen	['tɛmsən]
Rhine	Rhinen	['riːnən]
Danube	Donau	['dɔnaʉ]
Volga	Volga	['vɔlga]
Don	Don	['dɔn]
Lena	Lena	['lena]
Yellow River	Huang He	[ˌhwan'hɛ]
Yangtze	Yangtze	['jaŋtse]
Mekong	Mekong	[me'kɔŋ]

Ganges	**Ganges**	['gaŋes]
Nile River	**Nilen**	['nilən]
Congo River	**Kongo**	['kɔngʊ]
Okavango River	**Okavango**	[ʊka'vaŋgʊ]
Zambezi River	**Zambezi**	[sam'besi]
Limpopo River	**Limpopo**	[limpo'pɔ]
Mississippi River	**Mississippi**	['misi'sipi]

83. Forest

forest, wood	**skog** (m)	['skʊg]
forest (as adj)	**skog-**	['skʊg-]
thick forest	**tett skog** (n)	['tɛt ˌskʊg]
grove	**lund** (m)	['lʉn]
forest clearing	**glenne** (m/f)	['glenə]
thicket	**krattskog** (m)	['krɑtˌskʊg]
scrubland	**kratt** (n)	['krɑt]
footpath (troddenpath)	**sti** (m)	['sti]
gully	**ravine** (m)	[ra'vinə]
tree	**tre** (n)	['trɛ]
leaf	**blad** (n)	['blɑ]
leaves (foliage)	**løv** (n)	['løv]
fall of leaves	**løvfall** (n)	['løvˌfal]
to fall (ab. leaves)	**å falle**	[ɔ 'falə]
top (of the tree)	**tretopp** (m)	['trɛˌtɔp]
branch	**kvist, gren** (m)	['kvist], ['gren]
bough	**gren, grein** (m/f)	['gren], ['græjn]
bud (on shrub, tree)	**knopp** (m)	['knɔp]
needle (of pine tree)	**nål** (m/f)	['nɔl]
pine cone	**kongle** (m/f)	['kʊŋlə]
hollow (in a tree)	**trehull** (n)	['trɛˌhʉl]
nest	**reir** (n)	['ræjr]
burrow (animal hole)	**hule** (m/f)	['hʉlə]
trunk	**stamme** (m)	['stɑmə]
root	**rot** (m/f)	['rʊt]
bark	**bark** (m)	['bɑrk]
moss	**mose** (m)	['mʊsə]
to uproot (remove trees or tree stumps)	**å rykke opp med roten**	[ɔ 'rʏke ɔp me 'rutən]
to chop down	**å felle**	[ɔ 'fɛlə]
to deforest (vt)	**å hogge ned**	[ɔ 'hɔgə 'ne]

tree stump	stubbe (m)	['stʉbə]
campfire	bål (n)	['bɔl]
forest fire	skogbrann (m)	['skʊg,brɑn]
to extinguish (vt)	å slokke	[ɔ 'ʂløkə]

forest ranger	skogvokter (m)	['skʊg,vɔktər]
protection	vern (n), beskyttelse (m)	['væːn], ['be'ʂytəlsə]
to protect (~ nature)	å beskytte	[ɔ be'ʂytə]
poacher	tyvskytter (m)	['tyf,ʂytər]
steel trap	saks (m/f)	['sɑks]

to gather, to pick (vt)	å plukke	[ɔ 'plʉkə]
to lose one's way	å gå seg vill	[ɔ 'gɔ sæj 'vil]

84. Natural resources

natural resources	naturressurser (m pl)	[nɑ'tʉr rɛ'sʉʂər]
minerals	mineraler (n pl)	[minə'rɑlər]
deposits	forekomster (m pl)	['forə,komstər]
field (e.g., oilfield)	felt (m)	['fɛlt]

to mine (extract)	å utvinne	[ɔ 'ʉt,vinə]
mining (extraction)	utvinning (m/f)	['ʉt,viniŋ]
ore	malm (m)	['mɑlm]
mine (e.g., for coal)	gruve (m/f)	['grʉvə]
shaft (mine ~)	gruvesjakt (m/f)	['grʉvə,ʂɑkt]
miner	gruvearbeider (m)	['grʉvə'ar,bæjdər]

gas (natural ~)	gass (m)	['gɑs]
gas pipeline	gassledning (m)	['gɑs,ledniŋ]

oil (petroleum)	olje (m)	['ɔljə]
oil pipeline	oljeledning (m)	['ɔljə,ledniŋ]
oil well	oljebrønn (m)	['ɔljə,brœn]
derrick (tower)	boretårn (n)	['boːrə,tɔːŋ]
tanker	tankskip (n)	['tɑnk,ʂip]

sand	sand (m)	['sɑn]
limestone	kalkstein (m)	['kɑlk,stæjn]
gravel	grus (m)	['grʉs]
peat	torv (m/f)	['tɔrv]
clay	leir (n)	['læjr]
coal	kull (n)	['kʉl]

iron (ore)	jern (n)	['jæːŋ]
gold	gull (n)	['gʉl]
silver	sølv (n)	['søl]
nickel	nikkel (m)	['nikəl]
copper	kobber (n)	['kɔbər]
zinc	sink (m/n)	['sink]

manganese	mangan (m/n)	[ma'ŋan]
mercury	kvikksølv (n)	['kvik‚søl]
lead	bly (n)	['bly]

mineral	mineral (n)	[minə'ral]
crystal	krystall (m/n)	[kry'stal]
marble	marmor (m/n)	['marmʊr]
uranium	uran (m/n)	[ʉ'ran]

85. Weather

weather	vær (n)	['vær]
weather forecast	værvarsel (n)	['vær‚vaşəl]
temperature	temperatur (m)	[tɛmpəra'tʉr]
thermometer	termometer (n)	[termʊ'metər]
barometer	barometer (n)	[barʊ'metər]

humid (adj)	fuktig	['fʉkti]
humidity	fuktighet (m)	['fʉkti‚het]
heat (extreme ~)	hete (m)	['he:tə]
hot (torrid)	het	['het]
it's hot	det er hett	[de ær 'het]

| it's warm | det er varmt | [de ær 'varmt] |
| warm (moderately hot) | varm | ['varm] |

| it's cold | det er kaldt | [de ær 'kalt] |
| cold (adj) | kald | ['kal] |

sun	sol (m/f)	['sʊl]
to shine (vi)	å skinne	[ɔ 'şinə]
sunny (day)	solrik	['sʊl‚rik]
to come up (vi)	å gå opp	[ɔ 'gɔ ɔp]
to set (vi)	å gå ned	[ɔ 'gɔ ne]

cloud	sky (m)	['şy]
cloudy (adj)	skyet	['şy:ət]
rain cloud	regnsky (m/f)	['ræjn‚şy]
somber (gloomy)	mørk	['mœrk]

rain	regn (n)	['ræjn]
it's raining	det regner	[de 'ræjnər]
rainy (~ day, weather)	regnværs-	['ræjn‚væş-]
to drizzle (vi)	å småregne	[ɔ 'smo:ræjnə]

pouring rain	piskende regn (n)	['piskenə ‚ræjn]
downpour	styrtregn (n)	['sty:t‚ræjn]
heavy (e.g., ~ rain)	kraftig, sterk	['krafti], ['stærk]
puddle	vannpytt (m)	['van‚pʏt]
to get wet (in rain)	å bli våt	[ɔ 'bli 'vɔt]

fog (mist)	tåke (m/f)	['to:kə]
foggy	tåke	['to:kə]
snow	snø (m)	['snø]
it's snowing	det snør	[de 'snør]

86. Severe weather. Natural disasters

thunderstorm	tordenvær (n)	['tʊrdən‚vær]
lightning (~ strike)	lyn (n)	['lyn]
to flash (vi)	å glimte	[ɔ 'glimtə]

thunder	torden (m)	['tʊrdən]
to thunder (vi)	å tordne	[ɔ 'tʊrdnə]
it's thundering	det tordner	[de 'tʊrdnər]

| hail | hagle (m/f) | ['haglə] |
| it's hailing | det hagler | [de 'haglər] |

| to flood (vt) | å oversvømme | [ɔ 'ɔvə‚svœmə] |
| flood, inundation | oversvømmelse (m) | ['ɔvə‚svœməlsə] |

earthquake	jordskjelv (n)	['ju:r‚ʂɛlv]
tremor, quake	skjelv (n)	['ʂɛlv]
epicenter	episenter (n)	[ɛpi'sɛntər]

| eruption | utbrudd (n) | ['ʉt‚brʉd] |
| lava | lava (m) | ['lɑvɑ] |

twister	skypumpe (m/f)	['ʂy‚pʉmpə]
tornado	tornado (m)	[tʊ:'ŋɑdʊ]
typhoon	tyfon (m)	[ty'fʊn]

hurricane	orkan (m)	[ɔr'kɑn]
storm	storm (m)	['stɔrm]
tsunami	tsunami (m)	[tsʉ'nɑmi]

cyclone	syklon (m)	[sy'klun]
bad weather	uvær (n)	['ʉ:‚vær]
fire (accident)	brann (m)	['brɑn]
disaster	katastrofe (m)	[kɑtɑ'strɔfə]
meteorite	meteoritt (m)	[meteʉ'rit]

avalanche	lavine (m)	[lɑ'vinə]
snowslide	snøskred, snøras (n)	['snø‚skred], ['snørɑs]
blizzard	snøstorm (m)	['snø‚stɔrm]
snowstorm	snøstorm (m)	['snø‚stɔrm]

FAUNA

87. Mammals. Predators

predator	rovdyr (n)	['rɔvˌdyr]
tiger	tiger (m)	['tigər]
lion	løve (m/f)	['løve]
wolf	ulv (m)	['ʉlv]
fox	rev (m)	['rev]

jaguar	jaguar (m)	[jagʉ'ar]
leopard	leopard (m)	[leʉ'pard]
cheetah	gepard (m)	[ge'pard]

black panther	panter (m)	['pantər]
puma	puma (m)	['pʉma]
snow leopard	snøleopard (m)	['snø leʉ'pard]
lynx	gaupe (m/f)	['gaʉpə]

coyote	coyote, prærieulv (m)	[kɔ'jotə], ['præriˌʉlv]
jackal	sjakal (m)	[ʂa'kal]
hyena	hyene (m)	[hy'enə]

88. Wild animals

animal	dyr (n)	['dyr]
beast (animal)	best, udyr (n)	['bɛst], ['ʉˌdyr]

squirrel	ekorn (n)	['ɛkʉːɳ]
hedgehog	pinnsvin (n)	['pinˌsvin]
hare	hare (m)	['harə]
rabbit	kanin (m)	[ka'nin]

badger	grevling (m)	['grɛvliŋ]
raccoon	vaskebjørn (m)	['vaskəˌbjœːɳ]
hamster	hamster (m)	['hamstər]
marmot	murmeldyr (n)	['mʉrməlˌdyr]

mole	muldvarp (m)	['mʉlˌvarp]
mouse	mus (m/f)	['mʉs]
rat	rotte (m/f)	['rɔtə]
bat	flaggermus (m/f)	['flagərˌmʉs]
ermine	røyskatt (m)	['røjskat]
sable	sobel (m)	['sʉbəl]

marten	mår (m)	['mɔr]
weasel	snømus (m/f)	['snø‚mʉs]
mink	mink (m)	['mink]

| beaver | bever (m) | ['bevər] |
| otter | oter (m) | ['ʊtər] |

horse	hest (m)	['hɛst]
moose	elg (m)	['ɛlg]
deer	hjort (m)	['jɔːt]
camel	kamel (m)	[kɑ'mel]

bison	bison (m)	['bisɔn]
aurochs	urokse (m)	['ʉr‚ʊksə]
buffalo	bøffel (m)	['bøfəl]

zebra	sebra (m)	['sebrɑ]
antelope	antilope (m)	[ɑnti'lʊpə]
roe deer	rådyr (n)	['rɔ‚dyr]
fallow deer	dåhjort, dådyr (n)	['dɔ‚jɔːt], ['dɔ‚dyr]
chamois	gemse (m)	['gɛmsə]
wild boar	villsvin (n)	['vil‚svin]

whale	hval (m)	['vɑl]
seal	sel (m)	['sel]
walrus	hvalross (m)	['vɑl‚rɔs]
fur seal	pelssel (m)	['pɛls‚sel]
dolphin	delfin (m)	[dɛl'fin]

bear	bjørn (m)	['bjœːɳ]
polar bear	isbjørn (m)	['is‚bjœːɳ]
panda	panda (m)	['pɑndɑ]

monkey	ape (m/f)	['ɑpe]
chimpanzee	sjimpanse (m)	[ʂim'pɑnsə]
orangutan	orangutang (m)	[ʊ'rɑŋgʉ‚tɑŋ]
gorilla	gorilla (m)	[gɔ'rilɑ]
macaque	makak (m)	[mɑ'kɑk]
gibbon	gibbon (m)	['gibʊn]

elephant	elefant (m)	[ɛle'fɑnt]
rhinoceros	neshorn (n)	['nes‚hʉːɳ]
giraffe	sjiraff (m)	[ʂi'rɑf]
hippopotamus	flodhest (m)	['flʊd‚hɛst]

| kangaroo | kenguru (m) | ['kɛŋgʉrʉ] |
| koala (bear) | koala (m) | [kʊ'ɑlɑ] |

mongoose	mangust, mungo (m)	[mɑŋ'gʉst], ['mʉŋgu]
chinchilla	chinchilla (m)	[ʂin'ʂilɑ]
skunk	skunk (m)	['skunk]
porcupine	hulepinnsvin (n)	['hʉlə‚pinsvin]

89. Domestic animals

cat	katt (m)	['kɑt]
tomcat	hannkatt (m)	['hɑn,kɑt]
dog	hund (m)	['hʉn]
horse	hest (m)	['hɛst]
stallion (male horse)	hingst (m)	['hiŋst]
mare	hoppe, merr (m/f)	['hɔpə], ['mɛr]
cow	ku (f)	['kʉ]
bull	tyr (m)	['tyr]
ox	okse (m)	['ɔksə]
sheep (ewe)	sau (m)	['sɑʉ]
ram	vær, saubukk (m)	['vær], ['sɑʉ,bʉk]
goat	geit (m/f)	['jæjt]
billy goat, he-goat	geitebukk (m)	['jæjtə,bʉk]
donkey	esel (n)	['ɛsəl]
mule	muldyr (n)	['mʉl,dyr]
pig, hog	svin (n)	['svin]
piglet	gris (m)	['gris]
rabbit	kanin (m)	[kɑ'nin]
hen (chicken)	høne (m/f)	['hønə]
rooster	hane (m)	['hɑnə]
duck	and (m/f)	['ɑn]
drake	andrik (m)	['ɑndrik]
goose	gås (m/f)	['gɔs]
tom turkey, gobbler	kalkunhane (m)	[kɑl'kʉn,hɑnə]
turkey (hen)	kalkunhøne (m/f)	[kɑl'kʉn,hønə]
domestic animals	husdyr (n pl)	['hʉs,dyr]
tame (e.g., ~ hamster)	tam	['tɑm]
to tame (vt)	å temme	[ɔ 'tɛmə]
to breed (vt)	å avle, å oppdrette	[ɔ 'ɑvlə], [ɔ 'ɔp,drɛtə]
farm	farm, gård (m)	['fɑrm], ['gɔːr]
poultry	fjærfe (n)	['fjær,fɛ]
cattle	kveg (n)	['kvɛg]
herd (cattle)	flokk, bøling (m)	['flɔk], ['bøliŋ]
stable	stall (m)	['stɑl]
pigpen	grisehus (n)	['grisə,hʉs]
cowshed	kufjøs (m/n)	['kʉ,fjøs]
rabbit hutch	kaninbur (n)	[kɑ'nin,bʉr]
hen house	hønsehus (n)	['hønsə,hʉs]

90. Birds

bird	fugl (m)	['fʉl]
pigeon	due (m/f)	['dʉə]
sparrow	spurv (m)	['spʉrv]
tit (great tit)	kjøttmeis (m/f)	['çœtˌmæjs]
magpie	skjære (m/f)	['ʂærə]

raven	ravn (m)	['rɑvn]
crow	kråke (m)	['kroːkə]
jackdaw	kaie (m/f)	['kɑjə]
rook	kornkråke (m/f)	['kʉːnˌkroːkə]

duck	and (m/f)	['ɑn]
goose	gås (m/f)	['gɔs]
pheasant	fasan (m)	[fɑ'sɑn]

eagle	ørn (m/f)	['œːn]
hawk	hauk (m)	['hɑʊk]
falcon	falk (m)	['fɑlk]
vulture	gribb (m)	['grib]
condor (Andean ~)	kondor (m)	[kʊn'dʉr]

swan	svane (m/f)	['svɑnə]
crane	trane (m/f)	['trɑnə]
stork	stork (m)	['stɔrk]

parrot	papegøye (m)	[pɑpe'gøjə]
hummingbird	kolibri (m)	[kʊ'libri]
peacock	påfugl (m)	['pɔˌfʉl]

ostrich	struts (m)	['strʉts]
heron	hegre (m)	['hæjrə]
flamingo	flamingo (m)	[flɑ'mingʊ]
pelican	pelikan (m)	[peli'kɑn]

| nightingale | nattergal (m) | ['nɑtərˌgɑl] |
| swallow | svale (m/f) | ['svɑlə] |

thrush	trost (m)	['trʊst]
song thrush	måltrost (m)	['moːlˌtrʊst]
blackbird	svarttrost (m)	['svɑːˌtrʊst]

swift	tårnseiler (m), tårnsvale (m/f)	['tɔːɳˌsæjlə], ['tɔːɳˌsvɑlə]
lark	lerke (m/f)	['lærkə]
quail	vaktel (m)	['vɑktəl]

woodpecker	hakkespett (m)	['hɑkəˌspɛt]
cuckoo	gjøk, gauk (m)	['jøk], ['gɑʊk]
owl	ugle (m/f)	['ʉglə]

eagle owl	hubro (m)	['hʉbrʊ]
wood grouse	storfugl (m)	['stʊrˌfʉl]
black grouse	orrfugl (m)	['ɔrˌfʉl]
partridge	rapphøne (m/f)	['rɑpˌhønə]

starling	stær (m)	['stær]
canary	kanarifugl (m)	[kɑ'nɑriˌfʉl]
hazel grouse	jerpe (m/f)	['jærpə]
chaffinch	bokfink (m)	['bʊkˌfink]
bullfinch	dompap (m)	['dʊmpɑp]

seagull	måke (m/f)	['moːkə]
albatross	albatross (m)	['ɑlbaˌtrɔs]
penguin	pingvin (m)	[piŋ'vin]

91. Fish. Marine animals

bream	brasme (m/f)	['brɑsmə]
carp	karpe (m)	['kɑrpə]
perch	åbor (m)	['obɔr]
catfish	malle (m)	['mɑlə]
pike	gjedde (m/f)	['jɛdə]

salmon	laks (m)	['lɑks]
sturgeon	stør (m)	['stør]

herring	sild (m/f)	['sil]
Atlantic salmon	atlanterhavslaks (m)	[at'lɑntərhɑfsˌlɑks]
mackerel	makrell (m)	[mɑ'krɛl]
flatfish	rødspette (m/f)	['røˌspɛtə]

zander, pike perch	gjørs (m)	['jøːʂ]
cod	torsk (m)	['tɔʂk]
tuna	tunfisk (m)	['tʉnˌfisk]
trout	ørret (m)	['øret]

eel	ål (m)	['ɔl]
electric ray	elektrisk rokke (m/f)	[ɛ'lektrisk ˌrɔkə]
moray eel	murene (m)	[mʉ'rɛnə]
piranha	piraja (m)	[pi'rɑja]

shark	hai (m)	['hɑj]
dolphin	delfin (m)	[dɛl'fin]
whale	hval (m)	['vɑl]

crab	krabbe (m)	['krɑbə]
jellyfish	manet (m/f), meduse (m)	['mɑnet], [me'dʉsə]
octopus	blekksprut (m)	['blekˌsprʉt]
starfish	sjøstjerne (m/f)	['ʂøˌstjæːɳə]
sea urchin	sjøpinnsvin (n)	['ʂøː'pinˌsvin]

seahorse	sjøhest (m)	['ṣø‚hɛst]
oyster	østers (m)	['østəṣ]
shrimp	reke (m/f)	['rekə]
lobster	hummer (m)	['hʉmər]
spiny lobster	langust (m)	[laŋ'gʉst]

92. Amphibians. Reptiles

snake	slange (m)	['ṣlaŋə]
venomous (snake)	giftig	['jifti]

viper	hoggorm, huggorm (m)	['hʊg‚ɔrm], ['hʉg‚ɔrm]
cobra	kobra (m)	['kʊbra]
python	pyton (m)	['pytɔn]
boa	boaslange (m)	['bɔa‚ṣlaŋə]

grass snake	snok (m)	['snʊk]
rattle snake	klapperslange (m)	['klapə‚ṣlaŋə]
anaconda	anakonda (m)	[ana'kɔnda]

lizard	øgle (m/f)	['øglə]
iguana	iguan (m)	[igʉ'an]
monitor lizard	varan (n)	[va'ran]
salamander	salamander (m)	[sala'mandər]
chameleon	kameleon (m)	[kamələ'ʊn]
scorpion	skorpion (m)	[skɔrpi'ʊn]

turtle	skilpadde (m/f)	['ṣil‚padə]
frog	frosk (m)	['frɔsk]
toad	padde (m/f)	['padə]
crocodile	krokodille (m)	[krʊkə'dilə]

93. Insects

insect, bug	insekt (n)	['insɛkt]
butterfly	sommerfugl (m)	['sɔmər‚fʉl]
ant	maur (m)	['maʊr]
fly	flue (m/f)	['flʉə]
mosquito	mygg (m)	['mʏg]
beetle	bille (m)	['bilə]

wasp	veps (m)	['vɛps]
bee	bie (m/f)	['biə]
bumblebee	humle (m/f)	['hʉmlə]
gadfly (botfly)	brems (m)	['brɛms]

spider	edderkopp (m)	['ɛdər‚kɔp]
spiderweb	edderkoppnett (n)	['ɛdərkɔp‚nɛt]

dragonfly	øyenstikker (m)	['øjən‚stikər]
grasshopper	gresshoppe (m/f)	['grɛs‚hɔpə]
moth (night butterfly)	nattsvermer (m)	['nat‚sværmər]
cockroach	kakerlakk (m)	[kakə'lak]
tick	flått, midd (m)	['flɔt], ['mid]
flea	loppe (f)	['lɔpə]
midge	knott (m)	['knɔt]
locust	vandgresshoppe (m/f)	['van 'grɛs‚hɔpə]
snail	snegl (m)	['snæjl]
cricket	siriss (m)	['si‚ris]
lightning bug	ildflue (m/f), lysbille (m)	['il‚flʉe], ['lys‚bilə]
ladybug	marihøne (m/f)	['mari‚hønə]
cockchafer	oldenborre (f)	['ɔldən‚bɔrə]
leech	igle (m/f)	['iglə]
caterpillar	sommerfugllarve (m/f)	['sɔmərfʉl‚larvə]
earthworm	meitemark (m)	['mæjtə‚mark]
larva	larve (m/f)	['larvə]

FLORA

94. Trees

tree	**tre** (n)	['trɛ]
deciduous (adj)	**løv-**	['løv-]
coniferous (adj)	**bar-**	['bɑr-]
evergreen (adj)	**eviggrønt**	['ɛvi,grœnt]
apple tree	**epletre** (n)	['ɛplə,trɛ]
pear tree	**pæretre** (n)	['pærə,trɛ]
sweet cherry tree	**morelltre** (n)	[mʊ'rɛl,trɛ]
sour cherry tree	**kirsebærtre** (n)	['çisəbær,trɛ]
plum tree	**plommetre** (n)	['plʊmə,trɛ]
birch	**bjørk** (f)	['bjœrk]
oak	**eik** (f)	['æjk]
linden tree	**lind** (m/f)	['lin]
aspen	**osp** (m/f)	['ɔsp]
maple	**lønn** (m/f)	['lœn]
spruce	**gran** (m/f)	['grɑn]
pine	**furu** (m/f)	['fʉrʉ]
larch	**lerk** (m)	['lærk]
fir tree	**edelgran** (m/f)	['ɛdəl,grɑn]
cedar	**seder** (m)	['sedər]
poplar	**poppel** (m)	['pɔpəl]
rowan	**rogn** (m/f)	['rɔŋn]
willow	**pil** (m/f)	['pil]
alder	**or, older** (m/f)	['ʊr], ['ɔldər]
beech	**bøk** (m)	['bøk]
elm	**alm** (m)	['ɑlm]
ash (tree)	**ask** (m/f)	['ɑsk]
chestnut	**kastanjetre** (n)	[kɑ'stɑnje,trɛ]
magnolia	**magnolia** (m)	[mɑŋ'nʉlia]
palm tree	**palme** (m)	['pɑlmə]
cypress	**sypress** (m)	[sʏ'prɛs]
mangrove	**mangrove** (m)	[mɑŋ'grʊvə]
baobab	**apebrødtre** (n)	['ɑpebrø,trɛ]
eucalyptus	**eukalyptus** (m)	[ɛvkɑ'lyptʉs]
sequoia	**sequoia** (m)	['sek,vɔja]

95. Shrubs

bush	busk (m)	['bʉsk]
shrub	busk (m)	['bʉsk]
grapevine	vinranke (m)	['vin,rɑnkə]
vineyard	vinmark (m/f)	['vin,mɑrk]
raspberry bush	bringebærbusk (m)	['briŋə,bær bʉsk]
blackcurrant bush	solbærbusk (m)	['sʉlbær,bʉsk]
redcurrant bush	ripsbusk (m)	['rips,bʉsk]
gooseberry bush	stikkelsbærbusk (m)	['stikəlsbær,bʉsk]
acacia	akasie (m)	[ɑ'kɑsiə]
barberry	berberis (m)	['bærberis]
jasmine	sjasmin (m)	[ʂɑs'min]
juniper	einer (m)	['æjnər]
rosebush	rosenbusk (m)	['rʉsən,bʉsk]
dog rose	steinnype (m/f)	['stæjn,nypə]

96. Fruits. Berries

fruit	frukt (m/f)	['frʉkt]
fruits	frukter (m/f pl)	['frʉktər]
apple	eple (n)	['ɛplə]
pear	pære (m/f)	['pærə]
plum	plomme (m/f)	['plʊmə]
strawberry (garden ~)	jordbær (n)	['juːr,bær]
sour cherry	kirsebær (n)	['çiʂə,bær]
sweet cherry	morell (m)	[mʊ'rɛl]
grape	drue (m)	['drʉə]
raspberry	bringebær (n)	['briŋə,bær]
blackcurrant	solbær (n)	['sʉl,bær]
redcurrant	rips (m)	['rips]
gooseberry	stikkelsbær (n)	['stikəls,bær]
cranberry	tranebær (n)	['trɑnə,bær]
orange	appelsin (m)	[ɑpel'sin]
mandarin	mandarin (m)	[mɑndɑ'rin]
pineapple	ananas (m)	['ɑnɑnɑs]
banana	banan (m)	[bɑ'nɑn]
date	daddel (m)	['dɑdəl]
lemon	sitron (m)	[si'trʊn]
apricot	aprikos (m)	[ɑpri'kʊs]
peach	fersken (m)	['fæʂkən]

| kiwi | kiwi (m) | ['kivi] |
| grapefruit | grapefrukt (m/f) | ['grɛjp̩frʉkt] |

berry	bær (n)	['bær]
berries	bær (n pl)	['bær]
cowberry	tyttebær (n)	['tʏtə̩bær]
wild strawberry	markjordbær (n)	['mɑrk juːr̩bær]
bilberry	blåbær (n)	['blɔ̩bær]

97. Flowers. Plants

| flower | blomst (m) | ['blɔmst] |
| bouquet (of flowers) | bukett (m) | [bʉ'kɛt] |

rose (flower)	rose (m/f)	['rʉsə]
tulip	tulipan (m)	[tʉli'pɑn]
carnation	nellik (m)	['nɛlik]
gladiolus	gladiolus (m)	[glɑdi'ɔlʉs]

cornflower	kornblomst (m)	['kuːn̩blɔmst]
harebell	blåklokke (m/f)	['blɔ̩klɔkə]
dandelion	løvetann (m/f)	['løvə̩tɑn]
camomile	kamille (m)	[kɑ'milə]

aloe	aloe (m)	['ɑlʉe]
cactus	kaktus (m)	['kɑktʉs]
rubber plant, ficus	gummiplante (m/f)	['gʉmi̩plɑntə]

lily	lilje (m)	['liljə]
geranium	geranium (m)	[ge'rɑnium]
hyacinth	hyasint (m)	[hiɑ'sint]

mimosa	mimose (m/f)	[mi'mɔsə]
narcissus	narsiss (m)	[nɑ'ʂis]
nasturtium	blomkarse (m)	['blɔm̩kɑʂə]

orchid	orkidé (m)	[ɔrki'de]
peony	peon, pion (m)	[pe'ʊn], [pi'ʊn]
violet	fiol (m)	[fi'ʊl]

pansy	stemorsblomst (m)	['stemʊʂ̩blɔmst]
forget-me-not	forglemmegei (m)	[fɔr'glemə̩jæj]
daisy	tusenfryd (m)	['tʉsən̩fryd]

poppy	valmue (m)	['vɑlmʉe]
hemp	hamp (m)	['hɑmp]
mint	mynte (m/f)	['mʏntə]

| lily of the valley | liljekonvall (m) | ['liljə kɔn'vɑl] |
| snowdrop | snøklokke (m/f) | ['snø̩klɔkə] |

nettle	nesle (m/f)	['nɛslə]
sorrel	syre (m/f)	['syrə]
water lily	nøkkerose (m/f)	['nøkə‚rʊse]
fern	bregne (m/f)	['brɛjnə]
lichen	lav (m/n)	['lɑv]

greenhouse (tropical ~)	drivhus (n)	['driv‚hʉs]
lawn	gressplen (m)	['grɛs‚plen]
flowerbed	blomsterbed (n)	['blɔmstər‚bed]

plant	plante (m/f), vekst (m)	['plɑntə], ['vɛkst]
grass	gras (n)	['grɑs]
blade of grass	grasstrå (n)	['grɑs‚strɔ]

leaf	blad (n)	['blɑ]
petal	kronblad (n)	['krɔn‚blɑ]
stem	stilk (m)	['stilk]
tuber	rotknoll (m)	['rʊt‚knɔl]

| young plant (shoot) | spire (m/f) | ['spirə] |
| thorn | torn (m) | ['tʊːɳ] |

to blossom (vi)	å blomstre	[ɔ 'blɔmstrə]
to fade, to wither	å visne	[ɔ 'visnə]
smell (odor)	lukt (m/f)	['lʉkt]
to cut (flowers)	å skjære av	[ɔ 'ʂæːrə ɑː]
to pick (a flower)	å plukke	[ɔ 'plʉkə]

98. Cereals, grains

grain	korn (n)	['kʊːɳ]
cereal crops	cerealer (n pl)	[sere'ɑlər]
ear (of barley, etc.)	aks (n)	['ɑks]

wheat	hvete (m)	['vetə]
rye	rug (m)	['rʉg]
oats	havre (m)	['hɑvrə]

| millet | hirse (m) | ['hiʂə] |
| barley | bygg (m/n) | ['bʏg] |

corn	mais (m)	['mɑis]
rice	ris (m)	['ris]
buckwheat	bokhvete (m)	['bʊk‚vetə]

pea plant	ert (m/f)	['æːʈ]
kidney bean	bønne (m/f)	['bœnə]
soy	soya (m)	['sɔja]
lentil	linse (m/f)	['linsə]
beans (pulse crops)	bønner (m/f pl)	['bœnər]

COUNTRIES OF THE WORLD

99. Countries. Part 1

Afghanistan	**Afghanistan**	[afˈganiˌstɑn]
Albania	**Albania**	[alˈbɑniɑ]
Argentina	**Argentina**	[argɛnˈtinɑ]
Armenia	**Armenia**	[arˈmeniɑ]
Australia	**Australia**	[aʊˈstrɑliɑ]
Austria	**Østerrike**	[ˈøstəˌrikə]
Azerbaijan	**Aserbajdsjan**	[aserbɑjdˈʂɑn]
The Bahamas	**Bahamas**	[bɑˈhɑmɑs]
Bangladesh	**Bangladesh**	[bɑnglɑˈdɛʂ]
Belarus	**Hviterussland**	[ˈvitəˌrʉslɑn]
Belgium	**Belgia**	[ˈbɛlgiɑ]
Bolivia	**Bolivia**	[bɔˈliviɑ]
Bosnia and Herzegovina	**Bosnia-Hercegovina**	[ˈbɔsniɑ hersegɔˌvinɑ]
Brazil	**Brasilia**	[brɑˈsiliɑ]
Bulgaria	**Bulgaria**	[bʉlˈgɑriɑ]
Cambodia	**Kambodsja**	[kamˈbɔdʂɑ]
Canada	**Canada**	[ˈkɑnɑdɑ]
Chile	**Chile**	[ˈtʂilə]
China	**Kina**	[ˈçinɑ]
Colombia	**Colombia**	[kɔˈlʉmbiɑ]
Croatia	**Kroatia**	[krʉˈɑtiɑ]
Cuba	**Cuba**	[ˈkʉbɑ]
Cyprus	**Kypros**	[ˈkyprʊs]
Czech Republic	**Tsjekkia**	[ˈtʂɛkijɑ]
Denmark	**Danmark**	[ˈdɑnmɑrk]
Dominican Republic	**Dominikanske Republikken**	[dʊminiˈkɑnskə repʉˈblikən]
Ecuador	**Ecuador**	[ɛkʊɑˈdɔr]
Egypt	**Egypt**	[ɛˈgypt]
England	**England**	[ˈɛŋlɑn]
Estonia	**Estland**	[ˈɛstlɑn]
Finland	**Finland**	[ˈfinlɑn]
France	**Frankrike**	[ˈfrɑnkrikə]
French Polynesia	**Fransk Polynesia**	[ˈfrɑnsk polyˈnesiɑ]
Georgia	**Georgia**	[geˈɔrgiɑ]
Germany	**Tyskland**	[ˈtʏsklɑn]
Ghana	**Ghana**	[ˈgɑnɑ]
Great Britain	**Storbritannia**	[ˈstʊr briˌtɑniɑ]

Greece	Hellas	['hɛlɑs]
Haiti	Haiti	[ha'iti]
Hungary	Ungarn	['ʉŋɑːŋ]

100. Countries. Part 2

Iceland	Island	['islɑn]
India	India	['indiɑ]
Indonesia	Indonesia	[indʉ'nesiɑ]
Iran	Iran	['irɑn]
Iraq	Irak	['irɑk]
Ireland	Irland	['irlɑn]
Israel	Israel	['isrɑəl]
Italy	Italia	[i'tɑliɑ]

Jamaica	Jamaica	[ʂɑ'mɑjkɑ]
Japan	Japan	['jɑpɑn]
Jordan	Jordan	['jɔrdɑn]
Kazakhstan	Kasakhstan	[kɑ'sɑk‚stɑn]
Kenya	Kenya	['kenyɑ]
Kirghizia	Kirgisistan	[kir'gisi‚stɑn]
Kuwait	Kuwait	['kʉvɑjt]

Laos	Laos	['lɑɔs]
Latvia	Latvia	['lɑtviɑ]
Lebanon	Libanon	['libɑnɔn]
Libya	Libya	['libiɑ]
Liechtenstein	Liechtenstein	['lihtɛnʂtæjn]
Lithuania	Litauen	['li‚tɑʉən]
Luxembourg	Luxembourg	['lʉksɛm‚bʉrg]

Macedonia (Republic of ~)	Makedonia	[mɑke'dɔniɑ]
Madagascar	Madagaskar	[mɑdɑ'gɑskɑr]
Malaysia	Malaysia	[mɑ'lɑjsiɑ]
Malta	Malta	['mɑltɑ]
Mexico	Mexico	['mɛksikʉ]
Moldova, Moldavia	Moldova	[mɔl'dɔvɑ]

Monaco	Monaco	[mʉ'nɑkʉ]
Mongolia	Mongolia	[mʉŋ'guliɑ]
Montenegro	Montenegro	['mɔntə‚nɛgrʉ]
Morocco	Marokko	[mɑ'rɔkʉ]
Myanmar	Myanmar	['mjænmɑ]

Namibia	Namibia	[nɑ'mibiɑ]
Nepal	Nepal	['nepɑl]
Netherlands	Nederland	['nedə‚lɑn]
New Zealand	New Zealand	[njʉ'selɑn]
North Korea	Nord-Korea	['nʉːr kʉ'rɛɑ]
Norway	Norge	['nɔrgə]

101. Countries. Part 3

Pakistan	**Pakistan**	['pɑkiˌstɑn]
Palestine	**Palestina**	[pɑle'stinɑ]
Panama	**Panama**	['pɑnɑmɑ]
Paraguay	**Paraguay**	[pɑrɑg'wɑj]
Peru	**Peru**	[pe'ru:]
Poland	**Polen**	['pʊlen]
Portugal	**Portugal**	[pɔ:ʈʉ'gɑl]
Romania	**Romania**	[rʊ'mɑniɑ]
Russia	**Russland**	['rʉslɑn]
Saudi Arabia	**Saudi-Arabia**	['sɑʊdi ɑ'rɑbiɑ]
Scotland	**Skottland**	['skɔtlɑn]
Senegal	**Senegal**	[sene'gɑl]
Serbia	**Serbia**	['særbiɑ]
Slovakia	**Slovakia**	[ʂlʊ'vɑkiɑ]
Slovenia	**Slovenia**	[ʂlʊ'veniɑ]
South Africa	**Republikken Sør-Afrika**	[repʉ'bliken 'sørˌɑfrikɑ]
South Korea	**Sør-Korea**	['sør kʊˌreɑ]
Spain	**Spania**	['spɑniɑ]
Suriname	**Surinam**	['sʉriˌnɑm]
Sweden	**Sverige**	['sværiə]
Switzerland	**Sveits**	['svæjts]
Syria	**Syria**	['syriɑ]
Taiwan	**Taiwan**	['tɑjˌvɑn]
Tajikistan	**Tadsjikistan**	[tɑ'dʂikiˌstɑn]
Tanzania	**Tanzania**	['tɑnsɑˌniɑ]
Tasmania	**Tasmania**	[tɑs'mɑniɑ]
Thailand	**Thailand**	['tɑjlɑn]
Tunisia	**Tunisia**	['tʉ'nisiɑ]
Turkey	**Tyrkia**	[tyrkiɑ]
Turkmenistan	**Turkmenistan**	[tʉrk'meniˌstɑn]
Ukraine	**Ukraina**	[ʉkrɑ'inɑ]
United Arab Emirates	**Forente Arabiske Emiratene**	[fɔ'rentə ɑ'rɑbiskə ɛmi'rɑtenə]
United States of America	**Amerikas Forente Stater**	[ɑ'merikɑs fɔ'rɛntə 'stɑtər]
Uruguay	**Uruguay**	[ʉrygʊ'ɑj]
Uzbekistan	**Usbekistan**	[ʉs'bekiˌstɑn]
Vatican	**Vatikanet**	['vɑtiˌkɑne]
Venezuela	**Venezuela**	[venesʉ'ɛlɑ]
Vietnam	**Vietnam**	['vjɛtnɑm]
Zanzibar	**Zanzibar**	['sɑnsibɑr]